Beyond Separate Subjects:

Integrative Learning

at the Middle Level

Yvonne Siu-Runyan

&

C. Victoria Faircloth

Editors

with a foreword

by

John Lounsbury

CREDITS

LB
1570
. B49
1995
apr.1998

Every effort has been made to contact copyright holders for permission to reproduce borrowed material where necessary. We apologize for any oversights and would be happy to rectify them in future printings.

Chapters 1- 11

All student work included in these chapters is used with permission.

Christopher-Gordon Publishers, Inc.
480Washington Street
Norwood, MA 02062

Printed in the United States of America

10 9 8 7 6 5 4 3 2 1   99 98 97 96 95

ISBN: 0926842498

TABLE OF CONTENTS

Part III - Introduction

PREFACE

This book began with the coming together of two philosophies about teaching and learning. One focuses on the nature and curriculum needs of young adolescents; the other on the development of language and communication skills. Each targets the whole learner. One is specific about which learners, those endearing pubescents called "middle school kids." The other embraces a holistic view of language learning for all students.

When we started our conversations about what a book for holistic learning at the middle level should say, we realized we both had much to learn from the other. Although it was clear that our philosophies about teaching and learning overlapped, we needed time to discuss the terminology inherent in each field of expertise, and to explore the particulars of the middle school concept and the whole language movement in American schools.

A great deal of this occurred in Yvonne's home in Boulder, Colorado at a time when we were not distracted with other things. It was in that restful setting we had our grand conversations about what this book would offer to middle level educators. First, we discussed, debated, and reached consensus on exactly what the term "integrated curriculum" would mean in our book. Next, we examined the terms "middle school", "middle level," and "middle grades." After perusing the literature, we determined that these terms are often used synonymously. We agreed to use "middle level" in the title, but did not insist that term be used by chapter authors. From these decision points, the book began to take shape and develop a face of its own. It is our desire that this book provide for educators a view of integrated curriculum that begins with the thoughts, questions, and issues in the lives of young adolescents.

Using reading and writing to learn, inquire, construct, and examine ideas across the curriculum is central in an integrated curriculum. Helping young adolescents become competent readers and writers has unfortunately been isolated in many middle schools, and often falls upon the shoulders of the language arts/reading teachers. The fact that too many of our students do not view writing as a communication process that permeates the curriculum has led to severe under preparation of competent writers. Similarly, too many of our students do not view reading as an active, constructivist process where various perspectives can be examined and debated. This has led to students who read passively without much critical analysis of the text. We have added all kinds of "fixes" to these problems by asking students to keep journals about their learning, write summaries and essays, and read tradebooks to augment the textbook. The root issue here is that teachers are frequently not comfortable with writing themselves, nor do they understand that true comprehension occurs when readers share their understandings of the text and in the process extend each others' thinking about the text. The old adage that "we cannot take our students any further than we have gone ourselves" strikes an uncomfortable chord among many middle level teachers.

An integrated curriculum requires that all middle level teachers and students be readers, writers, thinkers, creators, explorers, and scientists. The challenge in developing integrated curricula is for teachers to relinquish ownership of content areas in order to create a whole curriculum. For integrative learning to happen, it takes a lot of self-determination, support from the administration, willingness to give up control, changing one's paradigm about separate-subject teaching, team-work, knowledge of the learner and content information, skill, and multiple resources. This book addresses each of these difficult issues.

While writing this book we experienced many emotions—fear, joy, hope, despair, frustration, and satisfaction. When teachers and their students work together developing integrated curricula, they too will experience these same emotions. We hope the ideas and experiences shared in this book give middle level teachers the confidence and tools necessary to meet the challenge of co-creating curriculum with their students.

YSR & CVF
February, 1995

FOREWORD

Twenty-five years ago it was said that the middle school was an idea whose time had come. Developments during the last two decades certainly indicate that such an optimistic affirmation was valid. The middle school movement, by nearly all accounts, has been remarkably successful. The number of new middle schools instituted together with the number of junior high schools restructured as middle schools have added up to a veritable revolution in school organization. The organizational battle, it would seem, has been won, although mopping up operations will continue for another decade or so.

But as middle level educators, while justifiably proud of the movement's success, have had time to reflect honestly on where they are in implementing the full middle school concept, in winning the big war to establish developmentally appropriate middle level programs, they recognize the larger campaigns yet to be mounted. All too often the early victories were largely organizational—grades included, name on building, schedule revisions, courses added—necessary prerequisites to other changes, but not the heart of the vision. Educational thinkers and leaders know that more is needed to create the best educational program for young adolescents.

Then, in 1990 Jim Beane published a small book, *A Middle School Curriculum: From Rhetoric to Reality*. It proved to be a watershed event. Bean's unapologetic critique of the separate subject curriculum, together with his setting forth an alternative approach to determining curriculum, quickly became a clarion call for the launching of a new offense. This publication seemed to be that probing needle that, on the one hand, forced honest assessment of the state of the middle school curriculum and, on the other, inspired and encouraged experimentations with more student-centered middle school curricula, ones based on what is known about learning and the needs of today's young adolescents.

In the four years since the first edition of Beane's book appeared, the pace of middle level curriculum reform has more than just quickened, it has exploded. Curriculum integration, it seems, is now the idea whose time has come. In contrast to the little movement relative to the curriculum itself during the previous twenty years what has happened since 1990 is truly remarkable. "Curriculum conversations" have been ongoing everywhere, and books and articles dealing with curriculum integration have become relatively numerous. And now this volume, *Beyond Separate Subjects: Integrative Learning at the Middle Level*, will readily and rightfully claim a place in this new genre of professional literature.

Moving from separate subject instruction toward curriculum integration, it should be recognized, is not just the latest pedagogical fad, simply another bandwagon that will elicit much publicity and several rounds of rhetoric only to fade from the scene in a few short years with almost no lasting legacy. The concept of curriculum integration has deep roots; it is anything but ephemeral or new. As this volume makes clear, its origins go back to John Dewey and even earlier. Considerable experimentation with integrative curriculum was successfully carried out in the 1930s and 1940s, primarily in the core curriculum movement. Then in the 1960s the middle school movement began to take hold and soon became the focal point for serious efforts to reduce departmentalization.

Now there is considerable evidence indicating that even in the midst of the contemporary conservative trend, a major reconceptualization of public schools' goals and curriculum is gathering momentum. This movement is essentially progressive and includes curriculum integration as a central element. Public dissatisfaction with the state of education, the lack of relationship between schoolwork and the contemporary concerns of youth and the needs of society itself are among factors that have led to widespread support for major educational reform. And what is already well underway in middle schools is now spilling over into the high school. Although these needed and fundamental changes will not easily or readily take place, their validity will keep them on the active agenda as old traditions and false assumptions fall under the intensity of the crises and the weight of evidence.

An important aspect, not always recognized, in these many efforts to go beyond separate subjects is their lack of uniformity. Wise teachers are not implementing "the" new curriculum, trying to put into practice somebody's proposed panacea. Rather, they are charting new ground based on where they are philosophically, where their students are in readiness, what resources are available, and so forth. While different, all involve students, engage them, and reduce the excessive degree of frontal teaching that has come to characterize most teaching.

This concept is well-illustrated in the chapters of this book. The approaches described are varied, but each one describes risk-takers, educators willing to step out and try something different, something that seemed to hold promise for improving the learning and development of their students.

The books is comprised of three sections, each with its own introduction. Section One contains two "foundational" chapters written by recognized curriculum scholars. The second section includes five chapters, all of which deal with a specific effort to integrate curriculum. The examples are relatively unique, unlike the more typical accounts of thematic units. The last section contains four chapters, all of which are varied in topic; but all offer information and support to those seeking to integrate curriculum.

All in all, *Beyond Separate Subjects: Integrative Learning at the Middle Level* is a rich resource, with a most interesting selection of chapters. It provides a good balance of philosophy and practicality and will be well-received by the growing groups of middle level educators who are seriously dealing with the too-long neglected aspect of the middle school concept—the curriculum itself.

John H. Lounsbury
Publications Editor
National Middle School Association
January 1995

Dedication

To ALL the middle school students and teach-

ers with whom we have worked. Thank you

for your dedication to young adolescents and

your inspiration to us.

YSR & CVF

Integrative Learning at the Middle Level: The Whys and the Whats

PART I — Introduction

I believe   that the active side precedes the passive
            in the development of the child nature;
            that expression comes before conscious impression;
            that muscular development precedes the sensory;
            that movements come before conscious sensations;

I believe   that consciousness is essentially motor or impulsive;
            that the conscious states tend to project themselves in
            action.

I believe   that the neglect of this principle is the cause of a large
            part of the waste of time and strength in school work.
            The child is thrown into a passive, receptive, or absorb-
            ing attitude.

- from *Dewey on Education* selections with an Introduction and
Notes by Martin S. Dworkin. New York, NY: Teachers College,
Columbia University, 1959, p. 28.

The first section of this book explains and clarifies the concept of
curriculum integration and why it is appropriate for middle school students.
This perspective is reinforced by Dewey's beliefs about the relationship
between child development and decisions regarding education.

In Chapter 1, Ed Brazee, former middle school teacher and now professor
of middle level education, aptly presents the need for middle school people
to think not only of organizational and climate issues, but to focus on the
curriculum itself. Brazee argues that curriculum needs to be responsive to
and aligned with the growth and development of young adolescents, and that
the kind of curriculum which has the greatest potential for meeting the
developmental needs of young adolescents is an integrated one. He states,

"It may seem odd that while the litany of growth and development issues are commonly cited as a need for a specialized middle school program, those same implications have NOT, until recently, been used as a rationale for middle school curriculum development. It is important to remember that actually using growth and development information to inform curriculum development is a return to our middle school roots."

James Beane, middle school curriculum theorist, identifies and dispels six myths that are associated with curriculum integration. These myths are those heard often from the general public, policy makers, parents, and even teachers. He nudges his readers to re-examine their own prejudices and perspectives about learning and suggests that involving middle level students in a meaningful curriculum can be achieved by moving away from separate subjects towards an integrated, holistic curriculum where students have a part in co-creating it with their teachers.

According to Beane, "Curriculum integration begins with real-life problems as themes, proceeds according to the organic integration of knowledge, and serves the purpose of enhancing self and world meaning." He further explains what it is not: "To be sure, the term 'curriculum integration' has been used to cover other moves beyond the strict subject-centered approach to curriculum, moves like multi-disciplinary and interdisciplinary arrangements as well as intradisciplinary correlations of sub-sets within such fields as language arts and science. Interesting as these may be, they begin with particular disciplines and almost always end with them, and for that reason they are simply not cases of the long line of work that is curriculum integration."

CHAPTER 1

An Integrated Curriculum Supports Young Adolescent Development

Edward Brazee

Room 202 at Brooks Middle School has a purposeful hum to it, reflecting the efforts of the community of learners who work there. A quick glance around the room shows clusters of students working together: one group sits on the carpeted floor critiquing questions for a survey on adult and young adolescent television viewing habits; another group huddles around several comput- ers as they complete a simulation on Westward Expansion; still others quietly ponder books or magazine articles; and a group of four stands at a chalkboard in the corner of the room, intently studying a large, schematic diagram of the local hydro-electric power plant.

A few moments later the teacher emerges from one of the groups on the floor and moves to a desk in the back where she has a clear view of the room. From this vantage point, she assesses the activities before her. Interestingly, no students approach her until she begins to move from group to group, listening to the discussions, observing and hearing about work in progress—a preliminary copy of the television survey, a summary of James Michener's views on the great rivers of the West—and, when asked, offers the name of a professor from the local university, an expert on hydro-electric power. It is obvious that students in this class know what they want and need to do. They are fully engaged in their own learning, serious, with a sense of purpose. It is also obvious that they genuinely enjoy their work, as they question each other enthusiastically.

While this scene could be a social studies or language arts class, it is a classroom with an integrated curriculum, where

*separate subjects are rarely identified and where students'
learning of content, skills, and processes far surpasses that in the
typical, separate subject classroom. Students study and work in
an atmosphere which more closely resembles a productive
office. In short, they know what they have to do, they know how
to get it done, and they are responsible for seeing that their work
is completed at a high level.*

*Students are excited about coming to school everyday
because they are involved in work that is interesting, difficult,
rewarding, and stimulating. This is not fluff or fun and games
time, although they and their parents originally thought that was
so. They do serious work, they learn a great deal of content as
well as needed skills, and recognize that they are responsible
for their own learning. Unfortunately, all schools aren't like this
one!*

For the past thirty years, preoccupation with organization and climate
issues has been the tail wagging the middle school dog. Surprisingly, the
excellent work of teachers and administrators committed to creating responsive schools for young adolescents has, until recently, not addressed curriculum to any significant extent. And this in spite of the fact that for 30+ years,
middle schools have made huge improvements in educating young adolescents (Lounsbury, 1984). The traditional way of thinking about curriculum
has been to regard it as merely another component of middle schools,
accepting its place alongside exploratories, advisories, teaching teams, and
other "middle school elements."

Instead, we must think of the *curriculum*, as encompassing every aspect
of the middle school; it is not an add-on, a stand-alone component which may
be added at any time in the conversion to middle school process (Brazee,
1989) or which is addressed only when organizational components of middle
schools are in place! Simply stated, as effective as the middle school
movement has been since the early 1960s in raising consciousness about
young adolescents and in providing responsive programs which meet their
unique needs, what the middle school curriculum *should* be has not been
addressed.

While the lists of middle school components (NMSA, 1982; Alexander &
McEwin, 1989) contain pieces of the larger curriculum puzzle—exploratories
and advisory programs, to name two of the most common—these and other
programs have been add-ons to the existing curriculum, not the curriculum
itself.

In many cases, the existing curriculum received little study and was either pushed-up from the elementary school or pushed-down from the high school. Other than several suggestions from middle school curriculum theorists (Arnold, 1985; Beane, 1975; Stevenson, 1986), discussion about what the "big picture" middle school curriculum should be has, until recently, received scant attention. For example, in compiling the chapters for *Reading in Middle School Curriculum—A Continuing Conversation* (Dickinson, 1993), the editor found only three articles on curriculum development in the middle school before 1985. The focus has been on separate programs and features which define the organization of new and converted middle schools.

Even though there are a number of different points which suggest a particular stance toward curriculum, the foundational rationale for middle school curriculum must be young adolescent growth and development. In her work with highly successful middle schools, Lipsitz (1984) found that a distinguishing feature of each school was its reliance on developmental appropriateness which informed every school practice. Stevenson (1992) refers to responsive education when our decisions about what to teach and how to go about presenting it are calculated on the basis of what we know about the multifaceted development of our students.

Cited as underlying features of middle school philosophy, physical, social, emotional, and intellectual development and the contexts in which they occur are frequently acknowledged in the literature, but less often applied in schools. That is, although developmental issues of early adolescence are cited as justification for the middle school concept, the implications of growth and development have rarely been applied to the middle school curriculum as a whole. While the need for strong adult guidance and opportunities to discuss issues critical to young adolescents is used as rationale for an advisor/advisee program, or for beginning an exploratory program, these same growth and development issues are rarely applied as the justification for evaluating, improving, or critiquing the curriculum.

In this chapter, I will explain how responsiveness to growth and development of young adolescents is the backbone of integrated curriculum. It may seem odd that while the litany of growth and development issues is commonly cited as a need for a specialized middle school program, those same implications have NOT, until recently, been used as rationale for middle school curriculum development. More importantly, we must remember that using growth and development information to inform curriculum development is a return to our middle school roots.

Finally, one of the most critical concerns as teachers study what the curriculum could and should be, is falling into the trap of "discarding" what has been done previously. While curriculum integration holds much potential for being truly responsive to young adolescent needs, some conventional instructional approaches found in separate subjects may be as effective. Similarly, some work offered in middle schools under the umbrella of integrated curriculum is totally inappropriate and is worse than traditional approaches. So, while curriculum integration may not be the total answer, it is at least one of the right questions. The very best elements of disciplinary teaching should be "planned into" integrated curriculum, and this includes both content and skills learning.

Integrated curriculum is not an exclusive term. Nor does it mean whatever anyone wants it to mean. Integrated curriculum brings together content, skills and attitudes in a manner meaningful to students and teachers. It uses students' natural proclivity to learn by focusing on their own questions, using content and skills as means to this end. While this is in contrast to the separate subject curriculum where students are often given chunks of content and skills which they have to assimilate, analyze, and synthesize, content and skills are critical pieces of an integrated curriculum as well. As complicated as these definitions have become, for the purposes of this chapter, integrated curriculum in its simplest sense means "making sense for young adolescents."

Understanding Developmental Needs

One of the happy coincidences adding strength and momentum to the early years of the middle school movement was the proliferation of information, research findings, and interest in early adolescence as a distinct phase of development. For the first time, 10-14 year olds were recognized as having unique needs and characteristics, different from those of children and older adolescents. When critics of the junior high school called for a school to more fully meet the needs of students, this increased attention to the period of early adolescence offered a compelling justification for the newly conceptualized middle school, a school to meet the unique developmental needs of this age group.

There are a number of excellent sources of information about growth and development issues which provide specific and useful information relative to the unique needs of young adolescents (Strahan & Van Hoose, 1988; Hill, 1980; Milgram, 1986), so it is not my intent to repeat that information here. There are, however, several caveats which are critical when considering the growth and development of young adolescents from ages 10 to 14.

Stevenson (1992) reminds us that because variability in physical growth, social adeptness, emotional needs, and intellectual development is so great, the extensive changes occurring in early adolescence can only be generalized:

- Early adolescence is a time when all youngsters change in many ways. The variety and pace of physical, social, emotional, and intellectual changes are well-documented, and it is accurate to say that young adolescents undergo more changes in these areas than at any other time of life.

- Changes occur at idiosyncratic times on a common schedule.

  Individual variability is the norm, as young adolescents move through changes in different parts of their lives at different rates and times.

- Home, neighborhood, and racial-ethnic identity influence development. Children whose parents listen to them, support their interests, and engage them in rational dialogue tend to be more likely to perform responsibly in school than those whose parents either ignore them or administer their authority dictatorially.

- The influences and effects of early adolescence are long-lasting. The myriad changes of early adolescence have long-term effects on personal adjustment.

One particularly useful framework for understanding the complex and continuous changes young adolescents undergo is published by The Center for Early Adolescence (1991), and it considers the developmental needs of early adolescents as the source of many challenges of this age group. To be effective, those who work with this unique group must remember that when referring to the developmental needs of early adolescents, no weakness or deficiency is implied (Stevenson, 1992).

Developmental Needs as Rationale for Curriculum

Based on extensive research of successful schools and community-based programs, and on a review of literature (Scales, 1991), The Center for Early Adolescence concluded that there are seven key developmental needs which characterize this age. Taken together, these seven needs focus on the positive goals for the healthy development of young people.

COMPETENCE AND ACHIEVEMENT

"Young adolescents need to find out what they are good at doing. They can be painfully self-conscious and self-critical and are vulnerable to bouts of low self-esteem, so they require varied opportunities to be successful and have their accomplishments recognized by others" (Scales, p. 14).

Simply put, young adolescents want to be competent, just as anyone does. They want to be successful in whatever they do and this includes academics, athletics, music, or any other interest areas. While the middle school has encouraged competence and achievement in areas outside the conventional curriculum—activity periods, exploratories, intramurals, and other programs—it is crucial to expand opportunities within the larger integrated curriculum as well, especially in those areas formerly dominated by the subject areas of science, mathematics, social studies, and language arts. Where in these separate subjects are there opportunities for students to be competent and achieve outside the traditional reading and writing assignments?

Sandra Caldwell (1992), principal of the Middle School of the Kennebunks (ME), frequently refers to the "dignity of expertise" which comes from being competent in a sport, music, a craft, or interpersonal relationships. Self-esteem does not exist separate from competence; self-esteem is a part of being competent. Thus, it is important to find the balance between academic pursuits and self-esteem. Not surprisingly, this is what the middle school has purported to be—a school with high expectations for learning and positive experiences for all students.

A distinction between academic and intellectual is critical here. While we differentiate between academic or non-academic, many of the "academic" activities may, in fact, involve little intellectual endeavor at all! For example, by virtue of their position in the traditional curriculum, such courses as language arts, science, social studies, and mathematics have "academic" status. In reality, though, the intellectual level may be quite low. Involving students in high-level thinking, problem-solving, and problem-posing while maintaining high expectations for their own involvement are examples of intellectual activities which promote learning. Sitting and listening to a teacher's lecture, dutifully completing worksheets or questions at the end of the chapter, or responding only to a teacher's directions are not academic. They require little or no intellectual activity or involvement. **As middle level educators, we should not confuse the appearance of rigor with real learning!**

The need for competence and achievement in all areas of their lives is essential for young adolescents because they must feel needed. They see adults succeeding, and they too wish to be recognized for their achievements. Often young adolescents feel left out; they are no longer children and yet are often treated as children; not quite yet adults, they have few of the privileges of adulthood. So, caught in this time warp between childhood and adulthood, it is especially important that young adolescents have opportunities to seek competence and achievement in learning at school.

Ironically, many young adolescents are very competent and have achieved a great deal in their young lives outside of school, through athletics, music, dance, or drama. We simply must take advantage of this developmental need by engaging them in meaningful learning and allowing them to be as passionate and enthusiastic about learning in school as they are out of school. Certainly, competence and achievement is an important element in an integrated curriculum because it reminds us to plan meaningful learning experiences, allowing young adolescents to demonstrate their competence and achievement.

Cognitive development suggests that young adolescents are beginning to develop the capacity for sustained higher-order thinking. For the first time, the possibility to think abstractly, to synthesize, and to pose problems and solutions appears. The integrated curriculum fosters higher-order thinking by involving students in learning, requiring them to think globally and to dissolve discipline lines by pulling together thoughts and ideas from various sources.

Meaningful Participation in Families, Schools, and Communities

"Young adolescents are intensely curious about the world around them, so they require exposure to situations in which they can use their skills to solve real-life problems. Young adolescents need to participate in the activities that shape their lives" (Scales, p. 14).

If any one thing could be said about the conventional curriculum it would be that it is boring (Arnold, 1991). It is something that happens *to*, not *with*, young adolescents at a time in their lives when they desperately want to contribute in meaningful ways. Content is doled out in bits and pieces with little attachment to the whole. And because content is "owned" by different subject areas, students rarely see the larger picture.

By inference, much of the conventional curriculum is not meaningful for young adolescents. When we continue to ask them to sit for long periods with little engagement or involvement, and when they are asked to learn information and develop skills outside of a meaningful context, they have not fully used their capabilities.

Secondly, we continue to give young adolescents answers to questions they never asked or cared about, even when we know that they have compelling questions to ask of their own. Researchers in the Middle Level Curriculum Project (MLCP) reported the types of questions which a sample of 500 young adolescents in rural, urban, and suburban school districts posed. They illustrate the concern and the depth of thinking of young adolescents. The following are representative excerpts of student responses (McDonough, 1991):

- "I wish I knew how to start a recycling program in the community. I am very concerned about environmental problems."

- "I worry about my reputation and the earth. Both are in lousy shape."

- "I wish I knew why the world has so many problems and why the different countries just can't get along with each other. I wish I knew why people treat the earth the way they do, spraying aerosols into the atmosphere, ruining the ozone, burning trash, filling landfills, using up all our natural resources."

These are not frivolous questions. While many believe that left to their own devices, young adolescents would spend much of their time watching MTV and Beavis and Butthead, that is hardly the case. On the other hand, young adolescents will not usually ask about photosynthesis, the causes of the Civil War, long division, or algebra. But the good news is that they are intensely interested in many things. Several middle school curriculum writers (Beane, 1993; Brazee & Capelluti, 1994) suggest that these questions should form the basis for the middle school curriculum, one which allows meaningful participation in families, schools, and communities.

While some schools are working toward an integrated curriculum where such activities would be typical fare, other middle schools have given students opportunities to make real contributions through service learning projects. A number of these projects including H.U.G.G.S., the Paradise Project, and others are described by Arnold (1991) in *Visions of Teaching and Learning*.

An integrated curriculum allows young adolescents opportunities to become involved with their families, schools, and communities because it moves school beyond the four walls of the school building, allowing them to use "school learning" in authentic ways to solve pressing and real problems.

There is little doubt that we have a great underused resource in young adolescents, who are capable of so much and wait to be asked to contribute as active members of their society.

CREATIVE EXPRESSION

"Young adolescents need opportunities to express to the external world who they are on the inside, be that in music, writing, sports, art, cooking, or making up games for younger children to play" (Scales, p. 14).

The conventional curriculum has not addressed the developmental need for creative expression to any degree outside of separate, exploratory activities. Within the so-called "academic" curriculum, there is little concern for creative expression because it is often regarded as non-academic. Creative expression can and should exist in so-called "regular" classes, as well, with opportunities for students to study issues and answer questions in a variety of ways other than the typical reading and writing responses. Once again we must be creative and teach students how to respond through oral presentations, debates, position papers, technical writing, poetry, dance, drama, computer presentations, etc.

Gardner's Seven Intelligences (1987) framework and similar learning style information help us recognize that there are multiple ways to express knowledge and intelligence. Gardner posits different types of intelligences— linguistic, musical, logical-mathematical, spatial, bodily-kinesthetic, and personal (inter and intra)—which translate in many different ways for young adolescents to respond to important curriculum questions.

OPPORTUNITIES FOR SELF-DEFINITION

"Young adolescents are at a uniquely vulnerable time in their lives. They require time to reflect upon the new reactions they receive from others and to construct a consistent self-image from the many different mirrors in which they view themselves" (Scales, p. 14).

This developmental need is so important that it must not be relegated to a separate advisor/advisee program. Rather, it must permeate the entire curriculum. In integrated curriculum, learning is a balance between intellectual and personal development; there is no way to artificially separate the two. Also, an integrated curriculum encourages young adolescents to pursue questions which have meaning to them since these questions have both a personal component, ("How does that affect me?"), and a larger world view, ("How does that affect the world?"). In a survival unit, for example, students could read about various aspects of survival and could have opportunities to test themselves against others who have survived difficult situations. Reading about other young adolescents, having time to work with peers and adults, and generally just being in a supportive atmosphere of the team provide young adolescents with many opportunities to determine who they are.

POSITIVE SOCIAL INTERACTION WITH ADULTS AND PEERS

"Young adolescents identify with their peer groups' values and desperately want to belong, so they require opportunities to form positive peer relationships. Although they may not often admit it, they have a similar need for caring relationships with adults who like and respect them and who serve as role models and advisers" (Scales, p. 14).

In an integrated curriculum, young adolescents work closely with adults and peers in cooperative and highly collaborative, non-competitive settings. This arrangement transcends traditional teacher-student roles, because teachers and students are partners. Both are learners and teachers.

While the popular notion of adult-young adolescent interaction is typically thought of as a time of pulling away from adults, particularly from parents and teachers, this is hardly the case. Young adolescents want to know that their parents and teachers are nearby, perhaps around the corner, so that they are there when needed. On-going, consistent, and caring relationships between students and adults in the school setting are critical components of the integrated curriculum. Opportunities to work with peers and adults on topics of high interest are especially compelling.

Perhaps the best way to visualize the positive possibilities of such close relationships with adults is to consider something different. Many middle schools recognizing the developmental needs of young adolescents have replaced the current system of short duration, random, formal teacher-student contacts, which usually result in only a superficial and formal working relationship, with a different one. This different organizational model facilitates curriculum integration by keeping teams of teachers and students together for several years.

PHYSICAL ACTIVITY

"Young adolescents experience very rapid and uneven physical development. They have a tremendous amount of energy, so they require a great deal of physical activity and time for having fun, as well as time for relaxation" (Scales, p. 14).

The integrated curriculum provides many opportunities for physical activity, both formally and informally. The chance to move about the room as needed when working is a privilege which many young adolescents have never experienced. Since an integrated curriculum is typically more flexible, breaks can be taken so that young adolescent bodies do not spend large amounts of time, sitting in one position. Young adolescents are interested in the changes occurring in their bodies, and they should have opportunties to learn about these changes. *Turning Points: Preparing American Youth for the 21st Century* (1989) and subsequent reports focus on the health of young adolescents, at a time when health needs are most acute. When bodies are changing, sleep, diet, exercise, and movement are especially critical considerations

STRUCTURE AND CLEAR LIMITS

"Clear expectations are crucial to unsure, self-critical young people. Explicit boundaries help define the areas in which they may legitimately seek freedom to explore. In their search for independence and autonomy, young adolescents often feel immune to risks and dangers, so they require structure and guidance in setting clear limits which allow them to participate in the decision-making process" (Scales, p. 14).

There are two key issues implicit in this developmental need. First, young adolescents do need assistance in setting boundaries in many aspects of their lives. Even those who appear older and hence more mature may have difficulty setting the limits they need. In an integrated classroom, it is not assumed that students automatically know how to set limits. They need frequent assistance and instruction when developing these skills. For example, setting realistic time limits for a task, deciding with whom to collaborate, determining what materials are needed, defining the purpose of the task, responding to the audience, and demonstrating mastery of the learning in question, are all key examples of the structures needed.

Second, their involvement in decision making is crucial. We can't expect young adolescents to know how to make decisions if we have not given them opportunities to do so. The nature of an integrated curriculum, like life itself, requires a complex series of decisions to be made:

- What questions am I interested in studying?
- How can I best answer those questions?
- What materials should I use?
- How will I know when I have answered my questions?

Finally, it is important to recognize that the developmental need for structure and clear limits is critical for young adolescents. An integrated curriculum is often *perceived* as being unstructured, a "do your own thing" activity, yet this couldn't be further from the truth. While the integrated curriculum looks "different" from that in conventional classrooms, it actually requires a greater amount of structure than the traditional classroom environment. Why is this so? Because there is a great deal of small group and independent work rather than everyone doing the same thing at the same time. Also, students share responsibility for their learning and thus are empowered to make many decisions which are not open to them in a traditional classroom.

While this type of classroom may look different than traditional ones, 30 students staring straight ahead at the teacher for 45 minutes everyday for 180 days, it more closely resembles a successful business or professional office where everyone has work to do and does it! In other words, time isn't necessarily broken up into short periods where isolated learning of content is the goal. Instead, there are large blocks of time to read, write, discuss, collaborate, question, and reflect, just as there are in real life.

This point is particularly important, for many perceptions of how schools and classrooms have to be come from our own experiences in traditional schools.

Moving Beyond the Traditional Curriculum

While there are numerous arguments for an integrated curriculum, perhaps the most compelling one is that an integrated curriculum best addresses the unique needs of young adolescents, yet is the least developed in practice. The developmental needs of young adolescents strongly suggest that many of the routine practices in middle schools—separate subject classes with no connection, rigid ability grouping, and random content and skill coverage—do *not* meet the needs of these same young adolescents (NMSA, 1992).

To meet the goals of developmental responsiveness, teachers, administrators, students, and parents must be willing to "take on" the most difficult area of the middle school—the curriculum. In the past thirty years, developmental responsiveness, the key issue of middle school education, has extended into most areas of the school *except* the curriculum. The usual scenario suggests that middle schools are developmentally responsive because they have advisor/advisee programs, because they are organized by teams, and because they offer numerous exploratory experiences. While these are important elements and are developmentally responsive, they stop short of addressing the heart of the school—its curriculum. Middle level schools have not lived up to their billing as developmentally responsive schools for young adolescents; they have failed to address the fundamental element of the school—its curriculum.

But, let's return to our scenario for a moment...

Integrated Curriculum in Action—
A Scenario Revisited

Students in this classroom at Brooks Middle School are studying a variety of topics clustered around a "survival" theme. Selected as the focus for study, this unit was developed using a curriculum planning process suggested by Beane (1990).

This type of student-teacher, collaborative, curriculum planning (Brodhagen, Weilbacher & Beane, 1992) requires students to pose questions they have about themselves and the world. Using group consensus and involving all students, questions are narrowed into thematic categories. Students in this class chose the "survival" theme because of their interest in: (1) the local power plant and its effects on the community; (2) whale research; (3) the survival of a particular species of seabird which had received a good deal of publicity at a local college; and (4) their own "survival" in the future, in ninth grade, in high school, and certainly later in life!

Next, students brainstormed possible activities which would allow them to answer their personal questions as well as questions about the larger world. A long list developed on all aspects of survival, including: reading and studying a plethora of materials on whales and their extinction; touring the power plant and interviewing key people in its employ; and investigating what life was really like in high school and beyond!

Finally, students brainstormed to determine the knowledge and skills that were necessary to answer their questions. Along with the expected requests to use reading and writing skills, students also wanted to use their skills in library research, problem-solving, note-taking, interviewing, prediction, vocabulary, map reading, and other areas.

This process is quite structured, and while it allows for input from students, it goes well beyond an "anything goes" mentality. Teachers fielded questions, clarified ideas, and encouraged further thinking, but they stayed in the background so that students' voices would be heard. Focusing questions for the unit, as agreed on by the class were:

1. What will be necessary for the planet to survive in the future?

2. What does survival mean to me? How did the people in *Alive* survive?

3. How did our ancestors survive? What were the biggest limitations to survival?

In addition to the teacher-student planning for this unit, all members of the school community met previously over a one year period to determine what the curriculum should be. In study groups, they read, discussed, argued, and deliberated over the essential question: What should the middle school curriculum be? This was not an easy process, but at the end, a document was produced which outlined the outcomes for students at Brooks Middle School. For the first time, parents, teachers, students, and administrators reached consensus on what was important for young adolescents to know and be able to do!

As described earlier, the day-to-day curriculum was devised around students' questions, yet, teachers knew what skills, content, and attitudes were to be learned. Traditional content and skills were interwoven in the process of answering students' own questions. Based on their understanding of growth and development issues (which they took seriously), the teachers wanted young adolescents to be high-level thinkers and they decided that an integrated curriculum allowed them to be just that.

Conditions Which Allow Integrated Curriculum to Be Successful

Changing the curriculum of the middle school means to fundamentally change the school for students, teachers, and parents. In this work, we must be careful not to appear arrogant or ungrateful for the fine work of teachers and administrators over the years, work centered primarily on organizational and climate issues. The time for fulfilling the original promise of providing a developmentally appropriate school which includes all aspects of the school, especially the curriculum, is now. Here are several issues teachers and administrators must act on as they endeavor to implement an integrated curriculum.

GREATER UNDERSTANDING AND ACCEPTANCE OF DEVELOPMENTALLY RESPONSIVE SCHOOLS

Even after 35 years, the general public (along with many educators) still does not understand the purposes, goals, and functions of middle schools. While it is inevitable that something new (like middle schools) takes time to be recognized and understood, it is also true that the entire K–12 continuum is not well understood either.

The larger issue requires us to assist parents and other members of the public in understanding what developmentally responsive education means. Although this involves a 180 degree shift in thinking, it is not a hard sell, especially to parents who recognize intuitively that their youngsters are not the same at 13 years as they were at age 8. While this knowledge seems easy enough to understand, making the requisite changes in schools to accommodate and provide for the type of school 13-year-old students need, is not easy.

We must simply stop talking about components of middle schools and talk first about developmental needs of young adolescents. If parents understand the underlying characteristics and needs of this age group, they will better understand the uniquenesses of the middle school, including its curriculum, as well as its organization and climate.

REDEFINITION OF TEAMS AND TEAMING

One of the most fundamental changes brought about by changing expectations for middle school curriculum is a drastic change in the concept of teams and teaming. Largely an organizational arrangement in many middle level schools, the Interdisciplinary Team Organization (ITO), was originally a way to break the departmental organization (from the high school) and brought together teachers from language arts, science, social studies, and mathematics. Although called a team, these teachers generally did their own thing, in their own classes, on their own time. An occasional "correlated" interdisciplinary unit, with a topic or theme carried out in four separate subject classrooms, contributed to keeping these teachers operating independently from each other.

Many teachers attempting to implement an integrated curriculum have found that smaller teams of 2-3 teachers are much more workable than 4-5 teacher teams, which remain largely subject focused. Some of these smaller teams have formed when teachers have broken away from the restrictions of larger teams.

But the size of the team is only half the story, because what teams actually do is the critical issue. High performing teams are critical to providing the structure for meaningful curriculum change. Effective teams require and nurture a tolerance for varying ideas. Just as we recognize student diversity in curriculum development, so should we honor and nurture it in adults (Brazee & Capelluti, 1995).

CHANGING ATTITUDES ABOUT *REAL* LEARNING

One of the major criticisms of *any* type of curricular change outside the conventional curriculum is that it does not involve serious and high-level learning. Much of this criticism is no doubt caused by those with a very limited view of what constitutes learning. The traditional school model— separate subject classes, seven-period days, teacher talk and student response, tests, and other school regularities—is recognized and regarded by nearly everyone as *the* model by which all other models are judged.

Students in schools involved in an integrated curriculum are learning in very different ways from traditional models. In these schools: (1) students identify their own areas of study, work cooperatively on them, and reflect on the entire process; (2) teachers have eliminated separate subjects; and (3) learning is organized into topics or themes which cross traditional disciplines.

An integrated curriculum offers more rigorous opportunities for learning than the conventional school curriculum. Students who work in an integrated curriculum find rigorous, intellectual learning, not "academic place-keeping."

RISK-TAKING IS NECESSARY

Not surprisingly, schools working with an integrated curriculum do so in different ways, at different points in their development as a middle school, and, of course, for a variety of different reasons. More significantly, teams within a given school function in vastly different ways in terms of their comfort and abilities with integrated curriculum. While Team A does not integrate curriculum much, concentrating on two multidisciplinary units in a year, Team B might designate half of its day as integrated block time with the other half devoted to separate subject classes. And team C might have a totally integrated curriculum based on student questions!

Wherever they are on the curriculum continuum, all teams begin with a "do-able" task and realistic expectations of what they can do. Largely, within the structures and parameters of their schools, each team changes from *within*. This is an important lesson!

Individuals in such schools are risk-takers, particularly in one important area—they do not wait for all questions to be answered before they begin their work.

A critical point which they all discovered is that, like the Nike slogan, they simply had to "just do it." There is rarely a magical movement when the planets are aligned or where a voice from a higher being urges us on. When it comes down to it, we must begin change at some point, even when things are totally set and when many of us are comfortable with the status quo. And yes, even when the test scores indicate that if "it ain't broke, why fix it!"

Much of change is contradictory. Go as far as you can at the beginning, but go slow enough so that you don't alienate too many people or leave them behind. Other change agents recommend to "push the envelope" as far as you can initially, because large changes become increasingly more difficult. Start large, start small, involve everyone, involve only those ready to change, and on and on and on (Horace, 1992).

Change must be of the heads-up, straight-ahead type where one realizes that we take risks and make professional judgments. This point cannot be stressed too much. Curriculum work is hard work and is not for everyone, but it is necessary and it does take thinking, reasoning, and a large degree of intestinal fortitude (Brazee & Capelluti, 1995).

CHANGING EXPECTATIONS OF TEACHERS AND STUDENTS

One of the greatest changes which results from putting an integrated curriculum into place is the altered roles of teachers and students. Instead of traditional, teacher dominant, student passive roles, their roles are now blurred as teachers become learners and students become teachers, as well as learners. This is much more than rhetorical, however, and underlies *all* aspects of an integrated curriculum.

Moving away from traditional roles takes a great deal of courage. For most of us it means setting aside the control we feel when in front of a classroom of young adolescents. It means not knowing all the answers; in fact it means not knowing all the questions! It also means that we should give away some of the responsibility for seeing to it that someone else learns and give it to the person who should be responsible, the learner!

Fulfilling the Promise

Nearly one hundred years after the first developmentally responsive school, the junior high school, it is time for the modern middle school to fulfill its original promise.

Appropriately, two elements must work in conjunction—knowledge about (1) young adolescent development and (2) integrated curriculum. While developmental appropriateness appears regularly as a rationale for various middle school components, it has rarely been used as justification for a focus on integrated curriculum. Ironically, the curriculum area has received little attention, given the excellent progress which middle schools have made in the areas of school climate and school organization.

Stated simply, we have come as far as we can by changing schedules, organizing teachers and students into teams, and adding on to the already over-crowded curriculum. Now we must turn our attention to crafting the curriculum into what it must be: responsive to the unique and compelling needs of young adolescents.

National Middle School Association's Middle Level Curriculum: A Work in Progress (1994), states what such a curriculum should be:

- All areas of knowledge and skill are important and are integrated throughout the student's school experience.

- Students explore integrated themes which engage them in serious and rigorous study.

- Curriculum is developed by careful and continuing study of students, social trends and issues, and research-supported school practices.

- Flexible learning groups are based upon students' needs and interests.

- Active collaboration and self-directed learning are encouraged.

- A variety of educational materials, resources, and instructional strategies are used.

- Staff development promotes and supports developmentally responsive practices.

- The staff is organized in ways that encourage ongoing collaboration.

- All staff help plan and participate in long-term professional growth opportunities.

REFERENCES

Alexander, W. M., & McEwin, C. K. (1989). *Earmarks of schools in the middle: A research report.* Boone, N.C.: Appalachian State University.

Arnold, J. (1985). A responsive currriculum for early adolescents. *Middle School Journal, 16*, 14–18.

Arnold, J. (1990). *Visions of teaching and learning: 80 innovative middle level projects.* Columbus, OH: National Middle School Association.

Beane, J. A. (1975). The case for core in the middle school. *Middle School Journal, 6*, 33–34.

Beane, J. (1990). *A middle school curriculum: From rhetoric to reality.* Columbus, OH: National Middle School Association.

Beane, J. (1993). *A middle school curriculum: From rhetoric to reality* (2nd ed.). Columbus, OH: National Middle School Association.

Brazee, E. (1989). The tip of the iceberg or the edge of the glacier: Curriculum development in middle school. *Mainely Middle, 1*, 18–22.

Brazee, E., & Capelluti, J. (1994). *Second generation curriculum: What and how we teach at the middle level.* Topsfield, MA: New England League of Middle Schools.

Brazee, E., & Capelluti, J. (1995). *Dissolving boundaries:Toward an integrated middle school curriculum*. Columbus, OH: National Middle School Association.

Brodhagen, B., Weilbacher, G., & Beane, J. (1992). Living in the future: An experiment with an integrative curriculum. *Dissemination Services on the Middle Grades, 23*, 1–7.

Caldwell, S. (1992). Speech given at the Middle Level Education Institute. University of Maine, Orono, ME.

Carnegie Council on Adolescent Development. (1989). *Turning points: Preparing American youth for the 21st century*. New York, NY: Carnegie Corporation.

Coalition of Essential Schools. (1992). What works, what doesn't: Lessons from essential school reform. *Horace Newsletter, 9* (2), 1–8.

Curriculum Think Tank. (1993). *Middle level curriculum: A work in progress*. Columbus, OH: National Middle School Association.

Curriculum Task Force. (1994). *Middle level curriculum: A work in progress* (2nd ed.). Columbus, OH: National Middle School Association.

Curriculum Committee. (1993). *Middle level curriculum: A position statement*. Topsfield, MA: New England League of Middle Schools.

Dickinson, T. (Ed.). (1993). *Readings in middle school curriculum: A continuing conversation*. Columbus, OH: National Middle School Association.

Gardner, H. (1987). Beyond the IQ: Education and human development. *Harvard Education Review, 57* (2), 187–193.

Hill, J. (1980). *Understanding early adolescence: A framework*. Carrboro, NC: Center for Early Adolescence. University of North Carolina at Chapel Hill.

Lipsitz, J. (1984). *Successful schools for young adolescents*. New Brunswick, NJ: Transaction Books.

Lounsbury, J. (Ed.). (1984). *Perspectives: Middle school education, 1964–1984*. Columbus, OH: National Middle School Association.

Lounsbury, J. (Ed.). (1992). *This we believe* (revised ed.). Columbus, OH: National Middle School Association.

McDonough, L. (1991). Middle level curriculum: The search for self and social meaning. *Middle School Journal, 23*, 29–35.

Milgram, J. (1992). A portrait of diversity: The middle level student. In J. Irvin (Ed.), *Transforming middle level education: Perspectives and possibilities* (pp. 16–27). Needham, MA: Allyn and Bacon.

Stevenson, C. (1986). *Teachers as inquirers: Strategies for learning with and about early adolescents*. Columbus, OH: National Middle School Association.

Stevenson, C. (1992). *Teaching 10–14 year olds*. White Plains, NY: Longman.

Scales, P. (1991). *A portrait of young adolescents in the 1990s: Implications for promoting healthy growth and development*. Carrboro, NC: Center for Early Adolescence, University of North Carolina at Chapel Hill.

Van Hoose, J., & Strahan, D. (1988). *Young adolescent development and school practices: Promoting harmony*. Columbus, OH: National Middle School Association.

CHAPTER 2

Myths, Politics, and Meaning in Curriculum Integration

James Beane

In some ways, it's surprising that there is a resurgence of interest in curriculum integration. While, this is an idea that is part of a long stream of progressive education with especially strong roots in the social reconstruction camp of progressivism, we are living in the midst of a conservative restoration. That socio-political movement has partly been constructed out of a harsh critique of progressive currents and a systematic dismantling of progressive social projects, including those that have been a part of the school curriculum (Apple, 1993). This is the era of school choice and vouchers, of neo-conservative character education, of challenges to sexuality education, of indoctrinate values education, of Channel One and the Edison Project. How could it be that an idea like curriculum integration, so long attached to progressive education, could catch the serious attention of so many educators in times like these?

There are, I believe, at least three answers to this question. First, the conservative restoration is not the only story of our age. Another is unfolding, both consciously and unconsciously, out of post-structural and post-modern theories of knowledge. This is a story partly characterized by a disillusionment with "truth." The tradition of "classical humanism," with its emphasis on a curriculum grounded in perennialist and presumably infallible knowledge, what Raymond Williams (1961) called the "selective tradition," is gradually giving way to more fluid and diverse views of knowledge. Herbert Spencer's famous puzzle for the curriculum field—"what knowledge is of most worth?"—is now less pressing in the curriculum field than the one drawn from political and cultural studies: "*Whose* knowledge is of most worth?" At the same time, Spencer's question is also under attack in terms of the late twentieth century knowledge explosion in which yesterday's knowledge is replaced by today's discoveries which may, in turn, be disproved tomorrow.

Second, while the gatekeepers of the dominant culture call loudly for a creed of homogeneous values, there is a simultaneous and powerful array of identity movements around race, class, gender, sexuality, and more, that pull mightily in the direction of heterogeneity. Despite their contradictions and tensions, these movements only strengthen the possiblity that what counts for official, high status knowledge will be dispersed across a wider terrain of viewpoints, and the formalized subjects that have so long paralyzed the curriculum will themselves begin to crumble. So may the elaborate mechanisms of centralized curriculum control, standardized tests, by-subject certifications, sterilized textbooks, and other vestiges of the pre-modern age that inhibit substantive curriculum reform.

Third, I sense a kind of restlessness among veterans in the profession, an uneasiness made of the disastrous effects of the conservative restoration on schools and society. Put plainly, many educators are tiring of rampant and radical individualism and its almost inevitable consequences of racism, poverty, injustice, and hopelessness. They seem to recall a time when their work felt like it had more meaning, when it might make a difference, when teaching had something to do with social progress and the common good. Now they wonder what happened to those days and whether they might be recaptured before teaching careers wind down. And, too, there are many young people entering the profession who want teaching to be about something more than technical implementation of standardized curriculum handed down from distant places. I do not want to overestimate the numbers of such people, but I sense that they are on the edge of what might be a critical mass.

I could be very wrong about all of this. It could be that renewed interest in curriculum integration is based on a poor or weak definition of its meaning and, consequently, that the term is only being used as another slogan in the midst of widespread school change that is merely symbolic and illusory. If that is so, then the remainder of this paper may well serve to take the glow off the current discourse around curriculum integration. But, if indeed the time is right—if curriculum integration is correctly seen as an opportunity to reclaim the half-forgotten legacy of democratic, problem-centered, constructivist curriculum—then perhaps what is discussed here will have some use. At some risk, then, I discuss what curriculum integration is about, addressing some of the myths that are attached to the way in which curriculum integration is defined and used, presently.

Myth 1: Curriculum Integration Has Many Meanings

Curriculum integration involves an idea whose American roots are best traced to John Dewey's pragmatic theory of the organic nature and instrumental uses of knowledge (c.f. Dewey, 1915, 1938). Its use in terms of the junior high school curriculum is widely regarded to have begun with the publication of *Integration: Its Meaning and Application* (Hopkins and Others, 1937) and subsequently to have reached prominence in the problem-centered core curriculum movement in the middle part of the century. It is in these sources and others like *The Integration of Educational Experiences* (Henry, 1958) that we find the three defining aspects of curriculum integration.

First, curriculum integration is grounded in the theory of integrative learning that is associated with the notion of the integrating personality. This theory posits that learning experiences are educative when they are integrated into the individual's present schemes of meaning about self and the world and, as such, both broaden and deepen those meanings *and* open possibilities for their continuous expansion. In this way, integration focuses its attention on the person who is learning, the meanings that s/he is constructing, rather than on externally contrived constructions of meaning.

Second, and related to the first, curriculum integration involves organizing learning experiences around real-life issues and problems rather than abstract disciplines of knowledge or other academic artifices. As Dewey (1915) pointed out:

> All studies arise from aspects of the one earth and the one life lived upon it. We do not have a series of stratified earths, one of which is mathematical, another physical, another historical, and so on. We should not be able to live very long in any one taken by itself. We live in a world where all sides are bound together. All studies grow out of relations in the one great common world. When the child lives in varied but concrete and active relationship to this common world, his (sic) studies are naturally unified. It will no longer be a problem to correlate studies. The teacher will not have to resort to all sorts of devices to weave a little arithmetic into the history lesson, and the like (p. 91).

We are left, then, with the question of what constitutes the contexts by which the "common world" is "bound together." Clearly they are not the artificial categories that make up disciplines of knowledge but the problems and issues that condition our collective lives and frustrate our shared aspirations. It is these problems and issues that focus our attention as organizing centers in curriculum integration.

Third, curriculum integration involves the organic integration of knowledge. The accumulated resources of the disciplines of knowledge are not ignored. Rather they are taken as one of the sources which are used instrumentally within the context of real-life problems. Put another way, resolution of the real problems of life depends in large part on the intelligent and creative use of knowledge. Such use, however, is only made more complicated and frustrating when that knowledge is differentiated by the socially constructed boundaries of distinct disciplines or, worse yet, their representation in separate subject areas (Beane, in press).

Taken together, these three aspects of curriculum integration create a particular meaning. Curriculum integration begins with real-life problems as themes, proceeds according to the organic integration of knowledge, and serves the purpose of enhancing self and world meaning. Such a description, of course, has a double edge. While it clarifies the meaning of curriculum integration it also uncovers other ideas that masquerade as curriculum integration. To be sure, the term "curriculum integration" has been used to cover other moves beyond the strict subject-centered approach to curriculum, moves like multi-disciplinary and interdisciplinary arrangements as well as intradisciplinary correlations of sub-sets within such fields as language arts and science. Interesting as these may be, they begin with particular disciplines and almost always end with them, and for that reason they are simply not cases of the long line of work that is curriculum integration.

Myth 2: Curriculum Integration Is An Instructional Technique

The preceding definition of curriculum integration, notwithstanding the overwhelming number of publications and workshops purporting to address the idea, seem to be concerned with making connections across the existing school subject areas. In this sense curriculum integration is taken to be a clever instructional technique. As we shall see, however, it is much larger than that.

To begin with, curriculum integration suggests a new epistomology for schooling. Following from Plato and Aristotle generally and in this country from the Committee of Ten (National Education Association, 1993), the public school curriculum has persistently been organized around a compartmentalized view of knowledge. Moreover, in the Western traditions of classical humanism and faculty psychology, this compartmentalized knowledge emanates from elite sources and is meant to be "banked" by passive learners (Freire, 1970).

Curriculum integration is about something very different from that tradition. Grounded in the theories of integrative learning and organic instrumentality of knowledge, curriculum integration works toward a democratic position of widespread and equitable participation in the uses and organization of knowledge as well as the construction of meanings. This is why, for example, curriculum integration involves localized collaboration of young people and teachers in curriculum planning rather than centralized, top-down planning. The classroom is thus more of a locale for the construction of meaning than a locale for the distribution of knowledge.

But more than this, curriculum integration in its authentic form is about social reconstruction. Quite frequently these days educators like to mention that they are using a "thematic" approach. Interesting as this claim might be, it does not tell us where the themes come from or what they are about. Usually, of course, such themes are content-embedded or, in other words, dragged out from within the existing subjects: "Colonial Living," "Middle Ages," or "Metrics." As we have seen, curriculum integration draws themes from life itself and, more specifically, problems, issues, or topics related to self and social meaning. Attention is focused on uncovering the conditions behind these problems with the aim of encouraging young people to be "critical readers" of their society. In this way, the work of curriculum integration intends to promote more than learning about such problems. It promotes the possibility of doing something about them.

Myth 3: Young People Will Not Learn As Much

Critics of curriculum integration claim that young people will not learn as much in that kind of organization as they do in a separate subject one, that there will be gaps, and that what is learned will not be of significance. I am tempted to dispense with this claim by simply asking, "How much are they learning now?" "Are there no gaps?" "Is whatever they are learning of great significance?" This would be an unkind response, since it reveals the embarrassing realities that lie just beneath the surface of what passes for curriculum in most schools as well as in most of the current symbolic curriculum reform efforts.

However, this myth is more complicated than that. It simultaneously reveals the widespread misunderstanding of curriculum integration and the intransigence of the subject centered approach. More than that, it is an incomplete sentence as it stands, begging for the question, "Learn as much of what?" If, for example, the question asks whether young people would "learn" as much of the kind of irrelevant and abstract trivia to which many are exposed now, the answer is no, they won't learn as much of that (as if they really learn it now).

The real problem with this myth arises from the misunderstanding that curriculum integration is about doing things differently rather than about doing something different. The purpose of the separate subject curriculum (as well as multi-disciplinary and interdisciplinary curriculum) is to disseminate and accumulate high status information in a form that reproduces the officially sanctioned differentiation of knowledge by subject categories. The purpose of curriculum integration is to broaden and deepen self and social, or world, meanings with an emphasis on constructivist and instrumental uses of knowledge.

Given these purposes, it is entirely likely that some of the content now held dear by subject loyalists, no matter how much beloved by them, may well be de-emphasized simply because its status in academic regimes cannot withstand the stiffer test of relevance to the personal and social affairs of people's lives. On the other hand, some of this subject material might well stand the test of relevance and significance, and in that way, enter fully into the approach of curriculum integration. In fact, the weight of the evidence in curriculum research falls heavily on the side of curriculum integration even with regard to subject driven measures. But more importantly, and again, the purpose of curriculum integration is not to accumulate such information. Comparisons of what young people learn in this arrangement compared to what they are taught in subject centered approaches are largely irrelevant because the two approaches are about different things. One fascinating result of such comparisons reveals the struggle of non-privileged young people as they encounter the obstacles constructed by gatekeepers of the dominant culture (Delpit, 1988; Beane, 1993).

Aside from this problem, which I do not want to underestimate, the questions arising from this myth are but one more example of misunderstanding about curriculum integration and the paralyzing effects of the separate subject approach. So deeply structured is the latter in the regularities of school life that too many people seem unable to even imagine any other possibility for the curriculum.

Those who cling to this myth simply do not see that the concept of curriculum integration is a curriculum. That is, the themes it involves and the processes by which they are carried out are in themselves what is to be learned and learned about. This kind of curriculum is not an empty cell.

Those engaged in it learn a great deal about themselves and their world, about building a sense of community, about collaborative planning, about critical readings of society, about real-life problem solving, and much more, including some of what is now languishing in abstract disciplines of knowledge.

I am tempted to simply dismiss this myth by saying that in curriculum integration, as just elaborated, young people will learn much more and about something different, yet more significant, than they do in the separate subject approach. But I am also aware that those who raise this criticism are clinging desperately to what is now covered regardless of its relevance to anything outside the narrowly proscribed subject curriculum that now prevails. In this sense, they are quite wrong about their making of the myth but at the same time quite right about the implication that their beloved content and its socially constructed sequences are almost inevitably at risk in something as powerful as curriculum integration.

Myth 4: Teachers Aren't Ready to Do This

This myth is, of course, false on the very face of it. If it were true, then there would be no cases of teachers working with curriculum integration in any schools. But since many are, we are compelled to try to understand what this myth is about and where it is coming from.

Teachers are by no means a monolithic group. Just as there are many teachers who are involved with curriculum integration, there are also many who are either unaware of its possibility or, being aware, unwilling to give it a try. Whatever the case, this myth works off the assumption that teachers have no control over their own work or ambitions. Such an assumption is not necessarily fictitious given the "deskilling" of teachers and "technization" of their work that has resulted from the increasingly centralized control of curriculum and other decision areas over the past two decades (Apple, 1986). However, it is a mistake to assume that teachers have no agency for progress or resistance in their professional work. If this is so, then how do we explain the significant efforts of progressive groups like Rethinking Schools in Milwaukee, the Boston Women's Teachers' Group, the National Council of Activist Educators, or Educators for Social Responsibility?

Notwithstanding that curriculum integration, done well, like any other curriculum approach, requires complex understandings and skills, this myth treats teachers in the same way that many young people are treated. That is, they are seen as unskilled, unknowing, and incapable. Clearly, then, this myth arises from somewhere other than teachers themselves, since it is hardly likely that teachers would willingly characterize themselves in this way. I'm suggesting that his myth might arise from those administrators and educational bureaucrats who are caught in the contradictory position of claiming that teachers should move ahead while at the same time wanting to control that movement. I want to be quite frank here in saying that those who claim that teachers aren't "ready" for curriculum integration, or for that matter anything else, are really saying that *they themselves* are not ready. This should come as no surprise, since curriculum integration means that there is hard work ahead for everyone inside and outside the school, work that involves undoing micro-mandates, schedules, certification regulations, textbook guidelines, testing systems, and virtually all other vestiges of linear, technical, and subject-centered curriculum organization, to say nothing of the price of commitment to progressive educational politics.

Before leaving this myth, we should note its corollary, "There must be steps along the way to curriculum integration." As I have previously pointed out, curriculum integration stands as a particular approach associated with a particular theory regarding learning, the uses of knowledge, and the sources of curriculum organizing centers. While falling under the general rubric of non-subject-centered design theories, it is substantively different from multi-disciplinary and interdisciplinary designs. The latter, then, are not "steps along the way to curriculum integration," but rather other alternatives to the separate subject approach. Moreover, that they are comparatively mild alternatives suggests that this aspect of the readiness myth has more to do with "nerve" than with the relations between curriculum theory and curriculum change.

I am reminded here of a remark made by a teacher that her teaching team had more difficulty moving from a multi-disciplinary approach to curriculum integration than from separate subjects to a multi-disciplinary approach. It was, she said, a case of being able to keep the separate subjects alive in the multi-disciplinary approach while having to "let go" of them in curriculum integration. In the end she thought it would have been much easier to move directly to curriculum integration, since multi-disciplinary work only delayed the inevitable.

The point of all this is that there are substantial numbers of teachers who are "ready" for curriculum integration, indeed many who are already deeply involved with it. The myth discussed here is little more than a thinly veiled prop to cover a larger failure of nerve by those educators who are unwilling to move ahead. Of course, if we allow the clever ploy of "waiting for everybody to be on board," we will probably all go to our graves before anything of significance happens.

Myth 5: Parents Will Object

There is perhaps nothing that will so surely strike fear into educators than the objections parents might make to a new approach. This is especially so at a time when the media relentlessly suggests that educators ought to be mistrusted, when right-wing fundamentalist groups elevate truth-twisting to a high art in order to preserve substantial gains in the larger Conservative Restoration of the 1980s. Given this scenario, widespread parental objection to curriculum integration may seem entirely likely. Yet for several reasons it is at least as likely, if not more so, that the large majority of parents will support curriculum integration.

First, it is not true that all adults had enjoyable or rewarding experiences in school and thus look fondly back upon the curriculum they experienced. One study, in fact, found that when asked to recall humiliating experiences from their youth, adults situated roughly two-thirds of those experiences in their middle level school years (Brenan, 1972). To argue, then, that parents would outright reject any school improvements suggests that they would deny their own histories or that they would want their own children to have similar negative experiences.

Second, numerous surveys over the years, such as those conducted annually by Phi Delta Kappa and the Gallup organization, have consistently found that parents place much higher trust in their local schools than in schools in general. The reason for this differential has simply to do with the difference between direct and vicarious experience. In other words, the localized stories of positive educational experiences of particular young people are more persuasive than the generalized lore of school failure.

Third, the history of how school authorities explain new programs to parents is not a pretty picture. If, for example, teachers wanted to explain curriculum integration to parents before trying it out, they would have nothing more to offer than a theory: "This year, your children will be involved in a new curriculum design in which themes are drawn from collaboratively identified personal and social sources and pursued without designation of separate subjects, in such a way that your children will understand instrumental uses of knowledge and experience authentic integrative learning." This kind of approach of "selling" a new program is nonsensical, yet typical of the way in which such matters are handled. Under these conditions, any of us would be likely to reject curriculum integration.

Parents want their children to have high-quality educational experiences, and they want them to do well. Yet through arrogance, misunderstanding, and carelessness, too many educators create exactly the kind of resistance that gives credence to the myth that parents will object. We have enough experience with curriculum integration, enough "success" stories (c.f. Stevenson and Carr, 1993), to know that parents will support the idea *if* they have an opportunity to see what it means for their children with regard to the comparative quality of other curriculum alternatives. When such stories, especially localized ones, are brought to light, this myth is almost always demystified.

I do not want to imply that building bridges with parents or the community-at-large will be successful or peaceful in all cases. The historically informed apprehensions of non-privileged parents aside, there are particular groups that may well persist in their objections to curriculum integration: right-wing fundamentalists, classical humanists, narrow academicians, and others whose interests work against progressive democracy, human dignity, and cultural diversity. However, objections from such sources must be seen and dealt with in political rather than in educational terms. To simply back away from such political conflict by avoiding curriculum integration is to deny young people the high-quality educative experiences that the majority of parents want for their children.

Finally, we might ask when it was that parental opinion so strongly swayed the curriculum decisions of educators. Not recently, or even much in the past. I, myself, have had three children go through middle level schools. Neither my opinion about how the curriculum should be organized nor my objections to the separate subject approach was taken seriously. More pointedly, would educators respond favorably if a group of parents demanded that reading and mathematics be abolished from the curriculum? I think not. Clearly this myth is more about the desires of educators than the apprehensions of parents.

Myth 6: All Young People Will Love Curriculum Integration

Since curriculum integration partly involves the search for self-meaning, it requires teachers to plan the curriculum with each particular group of young people with whom they work. Necessary as this requirement is, it also opens the approach to serious misunderstanding and unwarranted criticism. It seems that whenever teachers involve young people in curriculum planning it is automatically assumed that those young people will love it, because they were involved in planning with the teacher(s) what to learn. At the same time, critics of curriculum integration like to dismiss it on the grounds that it is nothing more than pandering to the immature whims of young people. Given the growing interest in curriculum integration, this myth, having the potential for trivializing and endangering this approach, is in desperate need of dissection.

To begin with, those of us who have been involved with curriculum integration do not ask young people what they are interested in or what they want to study. After all, curriculum integration is not about momentary interests, but rather about self and social meaning. Thus, our planning with young people involves helping them to clarify questions they have about themselves and the world as well as ways in which possible answers to those questions might be pursued. As reported elsewhere (Brodhagen, Weilbacher, and Beane, 1992), the kinds of questions that are raised generally engage powerful social issues rather than momentary and superficial whims.

That and other reports from classrooms (c.f. Stevenson and Carr, 1993) where curriculum integration is used suggest that this approach is more engaging for young people and that the number of disruptive incidents declines. However, curriculum integration is a theory of curriculum and not a theory of classroom discipline or management. We can change the curriculum, but we cannot so easily change the conditions or predispositions of young people. So, in classrooms where curriculum integration is used, as in other classrooms, there are young people who quite simply do not "love" what is going on.

The fact of the matter is that we live in a society where the lives of so many young people are threatened by degrading conditions of injustice, racism, sexism, homophobia, poverty, and so on that there will inevitably be young people whose attention lies somewhere other than on classroom matters. Moreover, by the time young people reach the middle level, some of them have had school experiences that are so demeaning we may be unable to attract their interest no matter what we do. And, too, there are those who have been taught to be so dependent on teacher-dominated, test-driven schooling that they are confounded by the relative freedom of curriculum integration.

In the end, though, curriculum integration is not aimed simply at gaining the affirmation of young people. Instead, it is a serious and rigorous attempt to have an educative experience for and with them. For those who wonder whether there will be discipline or management problems with young people, there remains the question, "How are things going now?" And for those who scoff at curriculum integration simply because it does tend to engage young people more fully than other approaches there is this question: "What would be the possible significance of a curriculum that does not?"

Conclusion

In this chapter, I have tried to dispel some of the myths surrounding curriculum integration and at the same time to reveal its meaning and the political implications of its use. The case I make may be summarized as follows.

- Curriculum integration involves a particular meaning for curriculum organization, learning, and uses of knowledge. Multidisciplinary, interdisciplinary, and intradisciplinary correlations are not examples of curriculum integration.

- Curriculum integration involves an alternative epistemology that is tied to progressive and constructivist education. It is not simply an instructional method.

- Young people will learn a great deal about significant matters in curriculum integration.

- Many teachers are anxious to undertake curriculum integration and understand that less dramatic alternatives to the separate subject approach are not steps along the way.

- Parents will not necessarily object to curriculum integration and may, for several reasons, be anxious to see it happen.

- While curriculum integration is likely to engage the attention of more young people than subject-centered approaches, some young people, for reasons quite apart from curriculum design theory, will find this no more engaging than other approaches.

These observations are not simply a matter or conjecture or blind faith. Rather, they emerge from what has been a long line of work on curriculum integration tied to the experiences of teachers and young people who have used this approach. That some people cling to the myths I have outlined has more to do with their own apprehensions than with the reality of authentic curriculum integration.

We have long stood at a crossroads that offers two paths. One is to define education as the acquisition of adult-selected, officially sanctioned information and meanings. The other is to turn ourselves over to an education that supports the organic and continuous search for self and social meaning. The two paths are not entirely mutually exclusive—at times they even converge. But the question before us is which we will choose for our major emphasis. We cannot simultaneously live fully on both paths. Nor can we simply bend one or the other to our own convenience, for this will only corrupt both and further confuse the meaning of education in our schools.

At present, a great deal of energy is being expended in symbolic curriculum integration. Most of this has to do with simply finding some themes to serve as a context for science, mathematics, literature, and so on, or tinkering with mild correlations among several subject areas. As we have seen, such efforts are not really about curriculum integration. Instead, they are about trying to find clever ways of repackaging our own interests. The history of curriculum reform tells us that such tinkering not only begs more crucial questions but makes the possibility of authentic reform less likely. It would be a sad thing, indeed, if the authentic meaning of curriculum integration were compromised in our own times and we had to wait 30 or 40 years for another moment of opportunity.

REFERENCES

Apple, M. (1986). *Teachers and texts*. Boston and London: Routledge and Kegan Paul.

Apple, M. (1993). *Official knowledge: Democratic education in a conservative age*. New York: Routledge.

Beane, J. (1993). *A middle school curriculum: From rhetoric to reality* (2nd ed.). Columbus, OH: National Middle School Association.

Beane, J. (in press). *Curriculum integration and the disciplines of knowledge*. Phi Delta Kappan.

Brenan, J. (1972). Negative human interaction. *Journal of Counseling Psychology, 19*, 81–82.

Brodhagen, B., Weilbacher, G., & Beane, J. (1992). *Living in the future: An experiment with an integrative curriculum*. Dissemination Services on the Middle Grades, *23*, 1–7.

Delpit, L. (1988). The silenced dialogue: Power and pedagogy in educating other people's children. *Harvard Educational Review, 56*, 379–85.

Dewey, J. (1915). *School and society* (rev. ed.). Chicago: University of Chicago Press.

Dewey, J. (1938). *Experience and education*. Kappa Delta Pi.

Freire, P. (1970). *Pedagogy of the oppressed*, M.B. Ramos, translator. New York: Seabury.

Henry, N. B. (Ed.) (1958). *The integration of educational experiences*, 57th Yearbook of the National Society for the Study of Education. Chicago: University of Chicago Press.

Hopkins, L. T., & Others. (1937). *Integration: Its meaning and application*. New York: D. Appleton-Century.

National Education Association. (1993). *Report of the committee on secondary school studies*. Washington, D.C.: US Government Printing Office.

Stevenson, C., & Carr, J. (Eds). (1993). *Integrated studies in the middle grades: Dancing through walls*. New York: Teachers College Press.

Williams, R. (1961). *The long revolution*. London: Chatto and Windus.

Integrative Learning at the Middle Level: The Specifics

PART II — Introduction

I believe   that education, therefore, is a process of living and not a
            preparation for future living.

I believe   that the school must represent present life—life as real
            and vital to the child as that which he carries on in the
            home, in the neighborhood, or on the playground.

I believe   that much of present education fails because it neglects
            this fundamental principle of the school as a form of
            community life.

- from *Dewey on Education* selections with an Introduction and
Notes by Martin S. Dworkin. New York, NY: Teachers College,
Columbia University, 1959, p. 22–24.

With an understanding of what curriculum integration is and is not, and
its relevance to middle level students, there are many considerations which
need to be addressed. In Section II, the "How To" of integrative learning is
discussed. For example, in order for curriculum integration to work well in
middle level schools, many important things must happen. There must be
administrative support at both the building and district levels. Teachers
must deal with changes that affect their personal and professional lives.
They must be able to work effectively together as a team. And, of course, they
need to learn how to take their lead from students as they co-create
curriculum and at the same time provide guidance and direction.

In Chapter 3, Norm Higgs, Bud Ashton, and Bernie Martinez, all
principals of middle schools where curriculum integration is being implemented, discuss the role the principal plays in facilitating integrative
learning. All too often, principals don't realize the strong influence they have
over the learning process of the teachers and, therefore, also learning of the
students as well. These administrators discuss critical insights regarding

support for teachers and issues of power that principals need to understand if they want teachers to integrate curriculum. Curriculum integration demands that both teachers and students are empowered to inquire about their own questions and figure out ways to find answers to those questions. Higgs, Ashton, and Martinez also point out that the staff development efforts cannot be a "flavor of the month" or a "project for the year" approach. Based on their experiences, they also warn how important it is to involve district office administrators, the school board, and the parents in this process.

Even though the principal may support and provide all kinds of encouragement to teachers, they still need to go through the change process themselves. In Chapter 4, Victoria Faircloth, a former middle school teacher and now professor of middle level education, discusses a number of assumptions about educational change. In addition she reviews the personal journeys of change which several teachers underwent when they worked with her on developing holistic, integrated curricula.

In Chapter 5, Tim Hillmer brings to light the many problems which occur when the human element of teaming is not dealt with. Because Hillmer is a middle school teacher and has faced many of the problems middle school teachers encounter when they try to integrate curricula, he offers concrete suggestions which will facilitate understanding, trust, sharing, relieve anxiety and fear, and build on people's strengths—all necessary ingredients if curriculum integration is to succeed.

In Chapter 6, Jan Kristo, a professor of language arts and reading, and Betty Robinson share how Betty goes about helping her students learn about the research process and how they investigate what students want to learn. Even teachers working with a team experienced with curriculum integration will gain a lot of insights from this chapter into how the language arts can be used in an integrated, holistic curriculum to sustain students' own inquiries and learning.

"Curriculum integration and learning by solving real problems go hand-in-hand." So begins Chapter 7, written by P. Elizabeth Pate, professor of middle level education, Elaine Homestead, middle school teacher, and Karen McGinnis, middle school teacher. The authors provide details about how they and their students went about co-creating integrated curriculum. The sample themes which took them through the entire school year demonstrate the power of involving students in a co-created, integrated curriculum throughout the entire school year. Notice how their year-long, holistic curriculum became more and more integrated as the teachers and students became more knowledgeable about the various aspects of curriculum integration.

CHAPTER 3

Facilitating Curriculum Integration: The Principal's Role

Norm Higgs, Bud Ashton, and Bernie Martinez

The popularity of curriculum integration continues to increase across the country. Strong advocates of the middle school concept herald integration as a way of looking at curriculum that has strong potential for providing students with learning experiences that are meaningful and help students connect what they learn with their lives. However, the old saying "talk is easy" certainly applies in this instance. Curriculum integration is one of the most difficult concepts to implement in schools because it requires teachers to re-think and reorganize their beliefs about curriculum and instruction. Implementing an integrated, holistic curriculum also calls for establishing a different kind of environment which may be foreign to teachers, students, paraprofessionals, support staff, and school administrators who have tremendous influence over school climate. Therefore, laying the groundwork is a necessary component in the process integrating curriculum. When doing this kind of preparatory work, it is most helpful for school administrators to ask themselves the following questions:

1. What are the pros and cons of a holistic, integrated curriculum in terms of student learnng? What does the literature say?

2. How will the central office administration be kept informed about where teachers are regarding their conceptualization and implementation about curriculum integration?

3. How will staff development be provided so that teachers are empowered to gain the knowledge and skills necessary for curriculum integration?

4. Does the school's organization allow for the flexibility and time needed in order to implement curriculum integration?

5. Has a decentralized decision-making process been established in the school in which teachers are allowed to explore new ways of teaching? Do the teachers themselves feel free to make those decisions?

6. Has the administration demonstrated support from the building and district levels that allows for curriculum integration?

7. Has curriculum been developed with outcomes that relate to curriculum integration?

8. Should there be changes in testing schedules, evaluating student performance based on rubrics or portfolios, grading student work, and reporting student progress to parents?

Thinking through questions like these are important first steps that the school administration must address before curriculum integration can happen. It is said, "The pack only runs as fast as the lead dog." Administrators who think that things will just happen because they want them to happen will often be disappointed. The process of moving forward with curriculum integration is not simple. It demands that aspects related to staff development, school organization and time, decision-making, building trust among the teachers, providing district support, having appropriate curriculum goals, designs and assessment procedures, and changing perceptions about learning and teaching be addressed, as well as having the active involvement of the school administration.

Staff Development

Teachers, parents, school board members, and administrators were schooled in an educational system in which a subject area was the basic focus of classroom instruction at the middle and secondary level. It is understandable that teachers would naturally refer back to their own experiences when providing instruction in the classroom. Thus, before asking teachers to accomplish the complex task of integrating curriculum, it is essential to understand that extensive staff development and time to accomplish the change are musts. A school should have a multi-year plan to allow for the staff to make the desired changes. Implementing a "flavor of the month" or a "project for the year" approach is not helpful when moving towards curriculum integration, for this kind of shift in teaching and learning demands changing perspectives, learning about different styles of teaching, and finding new ways of interacting with students in order to make their learning more constructivist, meaningful, connected, and holistic. Staff development should be centered not only on how to integrate curriculum, but also on exploring the whys and hows of reconstructing the school and rethinking the traditional subject-centered approach in order to support curriculum integration.

A word of caution. Before anything of substance can happen regarding curriculum integration, there needs to be commitment from the district to support it. It is most effective if district commitment is given early in the staff development process. It is also important for the district to have a plan for keeping all employees informed about the project.

PHASE 1: BECOMING KNOWLEDGEABLE (INITIAL INPUT—SUMMER IS BEST)

In the first phase, teachers and administrators should become knowledgeable about: (1) the philosophy of curriculum integration and how it will benefit students; and (2) the methods and techniques of instruction which support an integrated curriculum. This initial staff development program is most successful if it is not just a one-day, one-time occurrence. It should involve at least four or five days of training for the staff. We have found that a good way to start is to schedule a four- or five-day workshop during the summer when teachers are away from the time-consuming, intellectually taxing, and emotionally exhausting task of teaching.

In order to have some idea about the kinds of follow-up work teachers want and need for the second phase, it is important that teachers are asked such questions as: What aspect of curriculum integration are you struggling with? How can I help you answer your question(s)? What kind of help do you need?

PHASE 2: EXPERIMENTING AND SHARING WITH OTHER PROFESSIONALS (1ST AND/OR 2ND YEAR)

The second phase should provide opportunities for teachers to work together and experiment with the new ideas. In order to feel comfortable enough to risk moving toward a new paradigm of learning and teaching, teachers need follow-up in-service which supports their first attempts at teaming and curriculum integration. It is important that teachers do not work in isolation during this period of time, but are supported by other teachers. The forming of teams or study groups can provide this kind of necessary support. There needs to be an ongoing process of review and renewal of teaching practices during this time also. In order to support this review and renewal process, it is important that principals be knowledgeable of this approach and the intricacies involved. Principals who do not understand curriculum integration and its intricacies have difficulties providing teachers with the kind of human support needed in order to make and sustain change.

PHASE 3: HONING ONE'S SKILLS AND BECOMING A LEADER (2ND AND/OR 3RD YEAR)

During phase three, there needs to be a variety of on-going staff development and support. Administrators cannot assume that because teachers understand and support curriculum integration, they no longer need input and mentoring. This is the phase where teachers often are let down. Without continued support during this critical time, teachers often revert back to former teaching/learning approaches unless they are helped and supported. Such activities as peer coaching, attending state and national conferences and one-day workshops, and visiting other schools and chatting with teachers who are also working towards curriculum integration *all* have high pay-offs.

COMMON ELEMENTS IN PHASES 2 AND 3

During Phases 2 and 3, it is important for the principal to provide feedback to the teaching teams. Giving feedback to teaching teams can be done in several ways—attend team meetings and verbally share impressions, articles, and constructive feedback. This information can also be written down so that the team has a permanent record of the administrator's feedback. This kind of support helps teachers maintain a sense of security, provides an opportunity for teacher recognition, and develops a climate of teacher empowerment.

Also, during these two phases, it is essential that the principal provide a variety of assistance to teachers. Typical teacher requests are: extended planning time, especially when teachers in visual, technical, or performing arts are involved; additional supplies for student use in integrated projects; professional books and journals; and in-class, consultative assistance. Some teams may even request assistance in resolving an issue among team members.

School Organization and Time

The organization of the middle school provides a perfect structure for curriculum integration. Typically, middle schools are divided into teams which consist of 2–5 teachers and 50–125 students.

First, it is important for the organization of the school day to allow teachers to work together in order to integrate curriculum. Ideally, scheduling a block of time by combining four to six periods allows teachers flexibility in planning instruction. This is effective only if all students and teachers on the team are assigned to the same block of time. If either students or teachers must leave for another class, it ruins the opportunity for successful curriculum integration. *This block of time must also be one which is an uninterrupted learning time; school administrators must understand the need for large blocks of uninterrupted learning time and respect it.*

Second, giving teaching teams planning time is important and necessary. A school will not have long-term success at curriculum integration if team planning occurs before or after school. And just drop the idea that team planning will work at lunch! Time to formulate, discuss, and plan must be during the instructional day. If principals can give teachers both individual and team planning times, then curriculum integration has a better chance of succeeding.

Third, it takes *time* for teams to work towards curriculum integration. In most cases, teams work most effectively after being together for three years. For this reason, teaching assignments on teams should not be changed yearly. Why? During the first year, teams typically get to know each other, agree on common rules, grading procedures, and learn how to work as a team. Even after these issues are worked out, other issues occur which will need the team's attention. Cohesiveness within a team is important not only for the managerial aspects of teaching, but more importantly, team cohesiveness is necessary in order for people to work together in a synergistic fashion. Changing the team's structure without thoughtful consideration of all the ramifications only creates barriers to effective teaming and developing an integrated curriculum.

Some teams are more adventurous and begin to integrate curriculum in the first year together. Other teams will not be ready to do any curriculum integration during the first year, but feel more comfortable trying out an idea here and an idea there. Thus, it is important for the school administration to understand the different styles of working and provide enough time and organizational support during this critical period. Teams, comprised of individuals, should not be expected to look like one another nor work in the same way or by the same timeline. Without organizational support and enough time to explore and experiment without fear of repercussions from the administration, teachers will have little chance of success with curriculum integration. Given sufficient organizational support and enough time for planning, teams typically make greater strides with curriculum integration during the second year than in the first year. When this happens teachers are empowered, they have renewed energy, and they become excited about their accomplishments. This renewed energy and excitement, in turn, provide teachers with even more energy and courage to take the next steps on their journey towards curriculum integration.

Decision-Making

In W. Edward Deming's concept of quality organizations, he talks of decisions being made at the level where the work is being done (Aquayo, 1990; Gabor, 1990; Walton, 1986). This is especially true in education (Siu-Runyan & Heart, 1992; Wilson & Schomoker, 1992). Teachers who successfully integrate curriculum do this most effectively when they have a principal and a superintendent who are willing to allow them to make their own decisions about how the team should operate and what aspects of curriculum integration to take on.

Empowering teaching teams to make decisions without the principal's permission is a big step for administrators to take and often a scary one. We have found that one of the hardest tasks for a principal is to stay out of the way of teaching teams. The worst thing a principal can do is to reverse a decision made by a team, unless it is clearly inappropriate. Allowing teachers and teams to make decisions and live with their decisions, increases the chances of having a quality school, quality teaching, and quality learning.

Building and District Support

Being a change agent in a school district is enhanced if there is strong support at the building level and at the district level. Both the principal and the teachers need to be protected and supported when other staff members and the community start to question what is happening. Like anything new, the decision to integrate curriculum will draw criticism from those who believe that the curriculum should remain as it has been in past years. What are some things one can do to provide school and district support for curriculum integration?

- Support those interested in curriculum integration by providing a place where they can meet and where there are no distractions. Make it clear that anyone interested in pursuing this topic is welcomed. Do not set up a situation where there are the "in" group and the "out" group, the "haves" and the "have nots." Bring in guest speakers and order books and other professional resources on this topic. Be a part of this study group. It is important for the principal to be a learner right along with the teachers.

- During each phase of staff development, bring in the superintendent and/or the curriculum director and give them the opportunity to review progress and share in the energy and excitement that are taking place. In this way, central office personnel will gain a better understanding of how curriculum integration fits within the district's curriculum development efforts.

- Make it clear that you understand mistakes will be made by everyone, including the principal. Teachers need to be reassured that they will not be penalized when they try something new and fall on their faces. They need to know that the principal understands that when any new endeavor is undertaken mistakes are a natural by-product.

- Attend all in-services and actively participate by asking questions, offering suggestions, and sharing personal insights learned. Do not just introduce the speaker(s) and leave, only popping in from time to time throughout the in-service. This is not only distracting, it also gives the message that curriculum integration is not important. Besides, it is difficult to provide teachers with appropriate support if the principal does not know what teachers are learning, the questions they have, their comfort levels with curriculum integration, and the kinds of things they are struggling with.

- Once curriculum integration is on the way, make sure teachers receive recognition for their work. This can be accomplished at monthly parent meetings, school board meetings, in local newspapers, at school open houses, at staff meetings, in the weekly school newspaper, and by putting personal notes in teachers' mailboxes.

- Invite parents to a culminating activity at the end of the unit project review. This is a wonderful way to keep parents informed, garner their support, and provide visible support for student work, teacher teamwork, and curriculum integration.

When administrators engage in activities which demonstrate to teachers visible support, then accomplishing curriculum integration becomes a project which has an outstanding chance for success. After all, everyone needs a supportive community in order to take the risks necessary for change.

Curriculum Design and Assessment

Teachers worry about district requirements for which they are being held accountable. When the curriculum of a school district is structured around learning content of subject areas, it is difficult to integrate curriculum. Teachers are caught in a dilemma. They wonder, "How can I be accountable for the content of separate subjects areas and still integrate curriculum?" Thus, it is critical that the principal help district-level staff understand the kinds of curriculum changes that are needed in order to support curriculum integration. That is, the district's curriculum must reflect curriculum integration if curriculum integration is to succeed.

Teachers also worry about how they will evaluate their students. Because teachers typically focus on methods and techniques of instruction which support curriculum integration, they often put off thinking about assessing student learning. Because of this tendency, principals will need to review, research, and suggest assessment and reporting systems which are aligned with curriculum integration. To nurture empowerment, principals can encourage teachers to review and discuss the alternative assessment and reporting systems and select and/or modify the one(s) they feel are most appropriate for them and their students. As with other aspects of curriculum integration, the system of assessment and reporting that a team decides to use must be communicated to the students and parents.

Effecting Change in Attitudes

Without support from the public, it is difficult to sustain change. As educators, we must remember how important it is to help parents and the general public understand the rationale for curriculum integration. Parents and the public can be either advocates or adversaries. One way to build parent and public support for curriculum integration is to report evidence that it works. This can be done by presenting reports of success to other staff members and to other schools. Nothing will cause teachers to try a new approach or idea faster than a peer's testimony that something has worked.

Change does not happen overnight. It is a three- to five-year process which requires nurturing. School administrators need to understand that the teacher's role in the classroom and as a team member moving towards curriculum integration is *not* an easy transition. Therefore, nurturing and supporting people who are making the change is an important job the principal must do, for attitude is everything! When teachers feel supported as they move toward curriculum integration, the whole atmosphere in the school changes. We have documented this in the middle schools where we work.

Conclusion

If the perception is true that principals are ultimately responsible for everything that takes place in their buildings, then the evolution from teaching separate subjects to teaching an integrated curriculum can be traced to the level of commitment the principal has made to the curriculum integration process. Actions of principals must be aligned with their words; teachers should not be given mixed messages. To summarize:

1. Provide a variety of staff development opportunities and be a learner right along with teachers.

2. Don't expect changes to occur overnight; change is a three- to five-year process.

3. Allow teachers to decide for themselves how much change to take on and in what context, then support their decisions. Don't micro-manage.

4. Provide teaching teams time during the school day to plan.

5. Organize the school around large blocks of time. The typical 50 minute class does not facilitate curriculum integration.

6. Encourage experimentation. Let teachers know that mistakes will be made when trying anything new and that you understand this.

7. Help the district office understand that curriculum designed around separate subject areas defeats curriculum integration efforts.

8. Stay current with alternative assessment and reporting systems so that these systems can be used and/or modified to provide useful information to students, teachers, parents, and the district office.

9. Keep teams cohesive. It takes time to learn how to work with one another. Changing the make-up of teaching teams year to year actually inhibits curriculum integration.

10. Educate the parents and the larger community. Provide parents and the public with information about the benefits of curriculum integration. Showcase what the students have learned and why curriculum integration is a powerful way for middle school students to learn.

11. Realize that as a principal you will also be going through changes. Share your triumphs and defeats. Be a learner and a partner with the teachers.

REFERENCES

Aguayo, R. (1990). *Dr. Deming, the American who taught the Japanese about quality*. New York: Carol Publishing.

Gabor, A. (1990). *The man who discovered quality*. New York: Random House Times Book.

Siu-Runyan, Y., & Heart, S. J. (1992). Management manifesto. *The Executive Educator, 14* (1), 23–26.

Walton, M. (1986). *The Deming management method*. New York: Dodd, Mead & Co.

Wilson, R. B., & Schomoker, M. (1992). Quest for quality. *The Executive Educator, 14* (1), 18–22.

CHAPTER 4

Teachers and Students Taking Charge of Curricular Change

C. Victoria Faircloth

Over the past three years I have worked closely with middle level teachers and students in various schools throughout Colorado, investigating the concept of curriculum integration. From conversations and interactions with these teachers and students, some common attitudes, feelings, and experiences have emerged.

- *"The students are really into this integrated unit. They are taking charge of their learning."*

- *"I can see that this learning experience is more relevant to the students than what I had been teaching them."*

- *"It was awkward at first letting the students decide what they wanted to learn. I, as a teacher, was so used to making the decisions. It was definitely a new experience for me to watch the curriculum unfold as we (teacher and student) worked together on it."*

- *"At first I thought the kids would not learn what they needed to learn. But amazingly, they did learn what I thought they should have learned, and they learned a lot more than that too. They worked so hard on completing the projects. It was great to see them so excited about learning."*

From the comments, you might be asking the question: "Is integrated curriculum an idea that happened in these middle school classes without problems? Were there obstacles to change on the part of teachers and students? How did these people initially view the curriculum and what was the nature of the change process that brought about the implementation of an integrated curriculum?

This chapter will address the change process in the middle level curriculum from three aspects: the need for curriculum change, the nature of educational change, and the struggles and celebrations involved in successful change. Finally, conclusions are drawn as excerpts from personal reflections summarize teachers' experiences and validate the assumptions that frame this chapter.

The Need for Middle Level Curriculum Change

You have probably heard the saying, "Everything is closing in on me, and there's no place to go." For a young adolescent that means, "Physical, cognitive, social, and emotional changes are closing in on me, and there's no place to go but school!" Students in the age range of 10–14 experience all of these changes, sometimes concurrently, and are attempting to satisfy a set of curriculum goals imposed on them by a body of educational leaders in school district offices across the nation. During a period of great variability among students in terms of cognitive development, content-specific objectives abound in middle school curricula. The theory that students in the age range of 11-14 move to a formal stage of reasoning (Phillips, 1981) has been challenged in recent years by adolescent psychologists. It has been shown that approximately 80% of middle level students function at a concrete level of reasoning throughout their years in middle schools (Eson & Wolmsley, 1980). The vast amount of content knowledge which rests on the ability of students to think in abstractions forces us to face a serious dilemma—a mismatch of curriculum and learners. Curriculum that is based upon a given set of factual and conceptual understandings is not aligned with a population of students who are experiencing physical, cognitive, social, and emotional changes that rank second only to the changes that occur during infancy.

The work of Dewey (1916), and more recently the work of Beane (1993), suggest the need for a curriculum that is based upon the developmental nature of the young adolescent. Such a curriculum plan begins with learners, and is formulated to be relevant to the personal world of learners and to the problems and interests they find in the larger world around them. It is through meaningful educational experiences that students internalize what they learn, and "take it with 'em."

The case for curriculum change at the middle level has surfaced more than once over the last few decades. What holds educators back from curriculum reform? We hear arguments about competencies students must obtain and how America's students must be competetitive with other nations in learning information from specific content areas. These kinds of concerns have most definitely contributed to the argument against the development of integrated curricula. Despite these concerns, they are not, in fact, the major obstacle to curriculum integration. The crucial issue at stake in the argument regarding curriculum change at the middle level concerns *change* itself. Let us consider some assumptions about the process of change as they relate to middle level curriculum.

The Nature of Change

Assumptions about Change

Change is a part of all that occurs in our world. The impact that it has on education has only recently been viewed through the lens of the researcher. The pioneering efforts of Fuller (1969) paved the way for further studies regarding the nature of educational change. Theories regarding educational change have emerged largely as a result of national curricular reform efforts bombarding American schools in the mid-20th century. The post-Sputnik era of American competition in the cold war led to many large scale curricular reforms. Programs quickly fell by the wayside, only to be placed on the lowest shelf in teachers' bookcases. Curious about the fate of such grand curricular reforms, educational researchers began examining factors that might have contributed to the demise of these change efforts. As patterns arose, a number of assumptions emerged about the change process. A summary of these assumptions can provide the framework for a plan of action for schools in the transition from subject centered curriuclum to integrated curriculum.

1. *Change is a highly personal experience.* How educators manage change in the workplace is a personal experience. Some are eager to try new things. Others are more secure functioning within the subject matter boundaries for which they have been licensed. A few simply do not view change as needed or valued within the context of their teaching assignment. We cannot persuade our cohorts in education to change. We do well to consider the following quote: "Each of us guards a gate of change that can only be opened from the inside" (source unknown). So, cohersion might produce action on the part of teachers, but it does not produce curricular change.

2. *Change is a process—it takes time for change to occur* (Hall & Hord, 1974). Instant success is not a reality in education. Some

educators become impatient with educational innovations because they do not see immediate results. It is not uncommon to
hear in faculty meetings such statements as, "The kids aren't
learning any better with *this* philosophy about learning than
they did with *that* philosophy about learning." I have heard this
comment on several occasions when teachers and students had
been engaged in an integrated curriculum project for just a few
days! Any experienced teacher readily acknowledges that learning skills, concepts, and attitudes is time controlled. Learning,
whether it be to understand the mathematical concept of inte-
gers or to work on a problem-solving task with one's peers,
involves engagement for an amount of *time*. A different middle
school curriculum also involves learning on the part of teachers
and students. It requires engagement, or immersion for "x"
amount of time. No one can standardize it. Educators in middle
schools often have given up too soon, making hastily formed
judgments. If we develop long range plans with periodic check-
points, we will validate the inevitable struggles as part of the
process, rather than condemn the struggles as evidence of the
inferiority of the innovation.

3. *Change requires risk taking before all the data are in!* Educators
    cannot expect to know all the outcomes of curricular change
    efforts before changes are launched. Having the big picture in
    place can only come after some experience with change (Fullan,
    1991). Certainly, credibility for an innovation is gained through
    empirical and qualitative evidence, and an innovation should
    not be adopted before its success has been documented. How-
    ever, some investment must be made with students in the
    formative stages of an innovation. Data collection at various
    phases of implementation provides crucial information about
    the effects of change on learners. Formative assessment allows
    hypotheses to be refined and reformulated while students are
    immersed in the innovation. Pure and simple, the complexity of
    working with human subjects demands an approach that de-
    parts from the traditional idea of developing a plan, then follow-
    ing it to the end. Rather, we must embark on curriculum
    integration with the notion of "do, plan, and do and plan some
    more" (Fullan & Miles, 1992, p. 742).

4. *Change is learning, and it is surrounded with uncertainty.* As a
    process, change means dealing with the reality of creating new

personal meaning. Therefore, it becomes a learning process. Change involves risk taking. By risking change, we dethrone our comfort zones. The teacher becomes the learner. In other components of the middle level concept, middle level educators have been known for risk-taking behaviors. Examples include learning to work together on teams and the recognition of personal development as a critical component of the curriculum. We, the middle school community of educators, have waved the banner of student-centered schools. Banner waving creates excitement, but it doesn't effect curricular change. The next step awaits us, dethroning the comfort zone of the subject-centered curriculum. Our philosphy of student-centered schools for young adolescents must be exemplified in the curriculum that is delivered as well as in the curriculum espoused.

Considerations When Dealing with Educational Change

- *"The more things change, the more they stay the same."*

- *"Schools are constantly undergoing change. One new idea is replaced with another idea. Just hang on with teaching long enough, and this fad will pass too!"*

- *"I have been in teaching for 25 years, and nothing has changed. We just shuffle the same ideas around, giving them different names, so we can tell ourselves we're doing something new in education. It's all just a bunch of educational jargon!"*

You are no doubt familiar with some of these statements. Perhaps you have even said one or two of them yourself. On the one hand, we hear conversations about how everything is always changing. On the other, we hear that there is no change at all.

The literature on educational change suggests that a number of factors figure significantly into the success of educational innovations. First, they must be examined from the viewpoint of all participants (Hall & Hord, 1984; Fullan, 1991). This includes teachers, students, administrators, and parents. One cannot be expected to have ownership in a significant curricular change before learning about it. Process and product go hand-in-hand in curricular change.

A second consideration is the evidence that a large number of innovations have been implemented in fragmented and uncoordinated ways. Fullan and Miles (1992) note that individuals involved in reform efforts use "the maps" they are given to guide the change process. These "maps," which may include an operational definition of the innovation, an action plan, or a set of workshops on how to "do" the innovation, shape the implementation of an innovation and influence results. Therefore, those maps must be dependable, valid representations of what middle level curricular change looks like. Granted, the details are filled in as schools immerse themselves in the change process, but the maps must provide reliable guidance during this critical time of transition.

Educational change hinges upon teachers, not programs. Fullan (1991) speaks of the simplicity and the complexity of that statement. School districts may organize committees and task forces to examine curricular needs. Most of these groups include teachers. However, the point is that curricular change occurs when and only when teachers *make* it happen. The "think tank" meetings of higher education professionals, the challenging discussions of graduate education seminars, the carefully designed models, the detailed plans for implementation, all rest on what occurs with teachers and students in classrooms. The critical mass is in the practitioners. We must recognize their need to participate in training workshops, to interact with one another about their professional experiences, to develop mutual dependence through the sharing of struggles and growth. Nias, Southworth, & Yeomans (1989) state:

> Teachers are happiest in a social environment characterized by mutual dependence in which "sharing" is the norm and individuals do not feel ashamed to admit to failure or a sense of inadequacy... Relationships between staff who can and do help each other, provide one another with oases of calm in a long and frenetic day, set for one another high but attainable standards for professional performance, and provide a mutually supportive environment are characterized by personal accessibility; plenty of opportunity for discussion; laughter; praise and recognition (pp. 152–153).

Struggles and Celebrations in Successful School Change

University professors frequently do workshops for middle school teachers. Usually it is a one day, or half-day workshop, scheduled on an in-service day. We exchange ideas about topics such as the middle school concept with subtopics on components of the middle school concept such as teaming or curriculum. Time is provided for teachers to try out suggestions for classroom practice. At the close of the workshop, the teachers go home, and the professor goes back to the university to pick up mail, answer phone messages, and reflect on the effectiveness of the workshop. How does one assess the effectiveness of a one-day workshop? Can it be determined by how well you were received by the teachers? How about if you were organized and kept the workshop moving along on schedule? Or maybe you will know that the workshop was effective when and if the school invites you to do another one.

All too often, staff development workshops are given with similar considerations. However, it's important for us all to remember that the effectiveness of a workshop is determined by what teachers actually *do* in response to the ideas presented to them. Rarely does a workshop leader have follow-up with teachers. In-service days are one-shot deals that satisfy district requirements, but do little to sustain educational innovations. The administrator who plans for the success of innovations seeks consultation and mentoring for teachers on a *long-term basis*.

The teachers and principal of the South Valley Middle School in Platteville, Colorado, decided to investigate the notion of curriculum integration. They invited me to be the consultant. The principal and I discussed our options and agreed upon a year-long relationship between the school and myself. My time with the staff would be divided among blocks of time for instruction, which took the form of a course taken for college credit, bi-weekly meetings between each team and me, the implementation of an integrated project in each team that included a role for me (determined by team members), and some sessions for debriefing, evaluation, and planning for the future.

At press time, we are approaching the debriefing, evaluation, and planning phases of this year-long endeavor. The teachers would like you, the reader, to hear their voices of change as they embody personal experience, process, risk taking, and uncertainty.

Sixth Grade Project

The sixth grade project was a unit on cooperative learning. For a two-week period students learned rules to use in cooperative learning experiences. The last two weeks, the students developed a mini-society and applied the cooperative learning strategies learned during the first two weeks of the project. Team members are identified by the specialty area that has been their primary responsibility. In addition, a special education teacher and a Chapter 1 teacher collaborated on this project.

Sixth Grade Teacher Reflections

The main thing I worked on was being less bossy while working with the team. It wasn't as hard as I anticipated. I really like to have things my way, but I enjoyed working on myself to develop a more give and take attitude with my teammates. Now, handling uncertainties! My normal approach is to kick, scream, and have a tantrum, and then go for it knowing everything will turn out just fine. In this project, I was uncertain about two things. First, the team members' reluctance and philosophical differences about middle level curriculum concerned me, and second, I was concerned about my part in the teaching. We worked through several issues with major disagreements without any anger or hard feelings. I started with reservations, but I gained a deeper level of relationship with each of my team members.

- Julie Wilson, Special Education

*When a person goes forward into the unknown, it creates some caution and fear. Yet, some freedom to be creative and to experience success or failure can be stimulating. Most people do not wish to experience failure because it can be hard on the ego. But, when a sense of accomplishment can be felt and seen, what a rewarding experience that is for the ego! As I reflect on the project we did with the sixth graders, I must give credit to our principal for allowing us the freedom to explore curriculum integration without feeling fearful about launching out on a new experience. It is important to have the support of the leadership so teachers can function. Also, our consultant worked with us in the implemention of the project. Her participation in our team meetings ensured that we would remain focused and reach our objectives. When I allowed the students to work in their groups, I felt like things were not going as quickly as I expected. I had to talk to myself and explain to myself that the projects belonged to the **students**. It was not appropriate to lead them in the direction that I wanted them to go because they needed to depend upon themselves to solve the problems in their creative projects.*

- Dave Regalado, Chapter 1

It is important for me to be involved in something before I can understand it. So, our project was an opportunity to try out this concept. Sometimes it is difficult to inspire or motivate other team

members to try something new. Therefore, it was nice that this was presented as an all school project. I was comforted to know that we could start out conservatively and move toward an integrated curriculum. Uncertainties about this project were team related. Because I am a perfectionist, and somewhat compulsive, I found myself wanting to know for sure that all team members were equally committed to the project and that instruction across all classes was cohesive. I think that my role as team leader also contributed to my concern in this area, as well as the fact that I was uncertain about the level of commitment by the whole team. I was thrilled at the end of the project, though, by the many positive comments by our students. Some had found success for the first time all year!
- Judy A. DeAngelis, Language Arts

I must admit that I was reluctant and skeptical. My reluctance wasn't about integration, though. I think this is one idea that seems like a real way of changing middle school curriculum for the better. I was reluctant and skeptical about the worth of my role as a music teacher in this project. I figured everyone would tell me how music would work with their ideas, and then I would be asked to do some "fluff" teaching that was music oriented, like do a rap or play a song that was somehow related to our topic and call it integration of music into the project. This was irresponsible thinking. I realize that it was my job to ensure that my part in this project was meaningful and worthwhile for students. Another hesitation on my part involved my teaching in an area outside my formal training. I am an instrumental teacher and suddenly I was teaching general music because the students wanted to compose and sing national anthems for the mini-societies they had created. Yikes! Most people don't see a difference. However, it was very different than teaching band or orchestra. As I got into it, I realized that my love and enthusiasm for music, coupled with the knowledge I had, was more than adequate to help the students in their creative endeavors. I have learned to trust myself through this project. I gained more confidence in my ability to facilitate students' interests in all areas of music.
- John Jonas, Music Education

SEVENTH GRADE PROJECT

The framework for the seventh grade project was a study of the events surrounding the decades of the 20th century. Students on the team were asked what questions they had concerning these decades. Brainstorming sessions led to the development of small groups of students engaged in research in a decade of their choice, focusing on questions and concerns they had about that period of time. The project, guided by student inquiry, produced a variety of reflective responses from teachers. The interdisciplinary team was joined by the technology education teacher and physical education teacher for this student-driven integrated project.

Seventh Grade Teacher Reflections

I have learned through this project how important it is to allow the students to make their own decisions about how to display or share their learning. I worked with my students on a different level with this project. I backed off and allowed them to make decisions about their learning. Some of my students didn't run with the "popular" group. When they were allowed to work in a group of their own, their desire to learn blossomed. I had not given them the credit they deserved. I began to see them in a new light. They began to see me differently also. One student told me, "Mrs, Larson, I always thought you hated me. I thought you were too strict. Now I really like you and learned that it was just your personality." This made me feel good, but I realized that perhaps I had been too cold with my students so that they could not see the real me either.
- Leona Larson, Mathematics

I have a great deal to learn about facilitating student-driven learning. It is not a role that bothers me. I am not sure, though, that I was as helpful to the students as I could have been. I would like to observe some teachers as facilitators. During the time allotted for this integrated project, we gave up our team planning time to work with the students. Big mistake, in my opinion! We needed at least a couple of meetings per week. Some of our frustrations and uncertainties with each other came from a simple breakdown in communication, which could have been avoided.
- Raylene Olinger, Science

It was so rewarding to be a part of a student-driven learning project. Imagine the entire 7th grade working in the same room

(gymnasium) at the same time! It was hard sometimes not to say to my small group of learners, "We need to cover so and so." I had to remind myself that their issues had become the curriculum. It was also an opportunity to be a partner. Student-driven projects are exciting and scary because they are so open-ended. The scary part is the unknown—what will this look like? What are we supposed to make sure the kids have learned? They are guiding this, not us!! Do they realize the empowerment we have given them, or is it something they will realize when they think back on this experience? So many things going on in my head. The best part is the partnership and feeling of success for each participant. This integrated project has also brought six adults to the table to discuss a common goal or interest. We were actually "living learning." What an incredible opportunity for us to start at point A, continue to grow, re-examine, reflect, and improve. Yes! We are on the way to creating learning environments that are authentic, relevant, meaningful, and excuse me, but fun too!
- Pat Schaffer, Language Arts

Student-driven curriculum was an exciting challenge for me. Teaming has given me the confidence and the support system to go this far out on a limb and risk not being understood by colleagues and central office personnel. Any fears, doubts, or uncertainties that I had during this project came in the area of communication among the adults. I like to have every aspect of the unit thought through ahead of time. I am an ultra-conservative, rebellious, stubborn, New Englander! I feel that I don't do well in the people skills department. When working alone, I can do this at my pace and comfort level. When working collaboratively, I have learned that others do not need to have everything so "spelled out." I had to learn to relax a little and trust that everything would get done. I am one of those learners that wants to be told what to learn, so taking this risk with students was a little bit difficult because we were creating our own learning! At times I wondered if our principal thought the 7th grade team had left the ballpark because we wanted to allow the students to drive the learning that took place in our projects. My gut feeling is that integrated curriculum makes sense. I am not "married" to my content areas, and I don't understand why some teachers have such a difficult time with this. What is interesting, though, is that my first reaction to change is to be resistant. As a rule, I say

"NO!" first. I am not a "yes" person. But with every aspect of integrated curriculum I have readily, without question, accepted it. It makes so much sense! I can't see going back to the other way with middle school curriculum.
- Sheree Nale, Social Studies

Letting go of "our curriculum" was the most difficult for all of us. Trusting each other to pull our own weight, to fully participate in activities, was essential. Because of the uncertainty of the outcome, we had to create as we went along. We ran into conflict trying to fit curriculum needs, student needs, and our needs. We had made the decision to be a democratic community of learners. We empowered our students with the most valuable feature of our unit, which was taking charge of their own learning. The trust level of our students was heightened because the teachers did not have hidden agendas. We succeeded in communicating to students that there was no right or wrong way to arrive at an outcome. We abondoned our curriculum for this three week unit. Parents were involved in the assessment process. Students determined the scope of their learning. We conquered our own uncertainty and forced ourselves to take risks. Even though grades were given, the students never asked about them because they were learning what they wanted to learn.
- 7th grade project members: Pat Schaffer (Language Arts), Leona Larson (Mathematics), Raylene Olinger (Science), Sheree Nale (Social Studies), Kevin Carbaugh (Physical Education), and Brian McDivitt (Technology Education)

EIGHTH GRADE PROJECT

One of the critical learning experiences for eighth grade students was in the area of personal responsibility. The integrated project consisted of one week of instruction in personal finance, which was linked to decisions regarding career, marriage, and caring for children. The second week of instruction centered on the specific responsibilities of parenthood. Though not student-driven, the project was planned and implemented without discipline boundaries.

Eighth Grade Teacher Reflections

Earlier in my teaching career, I was more flexible and willing to try new things, usually rushing in, often without adequate prior planning and certainly not working closely with a team of

teachers. This time, I found it difficult and frustrating at times, as well as tedious and very time-consuming. I had to make sacrifices, take more risks, and work harder than I ever have before. When we began the implementation of the integrated project, I realized that all the frustrations, tedium, and sacrifices during the planning phase were going to be worth it. Our students were engaged, they were enjoying themselves, and they were learning. As team leader, I felt the responsibility of being a real listener, not pressing my opinions on the group, but recognizing when others' opinions and suggestions were worthy of merit, and at times, were a lot better than mine. My greatest area of concern about this project was that what we were doing for students might be a disservice to them because we were departing from the almighty district curriculum. I was also uncertain about how my lack of expertise would affect the project, even though I realized that everyone starts somewhere. I will always be somewhat conservative, but now, perhaps taking risks and having the confidence to stretch for new things and experiences, especially those that truly benefit students, will be easier. I like curriculum integration and look forward to more!
- Jon Billheimer, Science

I consider myself a private person and found it difficult to share with my teammates how I think, plan, work, and interact. I was frustrated when I perceived that students were being shortchanged for the sake of the structure of our integrated project. For the first time, I was forced to teach in a manner that wasn't mine. It seemed to me that sometimes we were making simple matters difficult. I risked opening myself to criticism and had to sacrifice what I thought was right, for the benefit of the team. When the project was completed, I was relieved to move on. I struggled with the nagging thought that expectations were not met and that sometimes the project focused on what the teachers thought would be fun, rather than focusing on what the students wanted to do and learn. I approach uncertainty with one foot mired in what I believe is right. Working with others is not my greatest asset. When placed in an uncomfortable position, I gather myself inward and listen and think. When the project was completed, I found the frustration was necessary, and enduring such proved worthwhile for students and teachers alike.
- Kristan Enright, Mathematics

When the eighth grade team began thinking of what to do for an integrated project, we brainstormed a multitude of ideas that could be developed from our various content areas, but we soon decided that we needed to get out of our "content ruts," and build something together. Although we had never taught together, I liked the idea of abandoning content areas. At first, I felt somewhat intimidated about sharing my ideas for fear that they would be considered mundane. It helped for us to do some team building first. We decided to focus on our strengths and weaknesses as a team, then focus on our individual concerns. We did this in a discussion session with our consultant present. Yes, we had been a team for several years. We had always discussed student issues, but for the first time, we were opening up to each other as professionals. I wondered if such a level of communication would be too threatening. Would my honesty make me seem ineffective to my team members? My biggest fear was being criticized by my fellow teachers. It was a relief to find out that we truly supported each other. The process required all of us to change. We had to trust each other and validate all ideas shared in our brainstorming sessions. We had to get away from the mold of the "old, experienced" teachers vs. the "young, in-tune" teachers. We were working together! The outcomes of the project were quite positive. Students frequently shared their enthusiasm with us by mentioning how much they had learned about life from the integrated project. Our team risked honesty and reaped camaraderie. We found that the voices of all of us were much stronger than the voice of one of us.
- Linda Gleason, Language Arts

Assumptions about Change Reflected in the Voices of Teachers

In this chapter, the change process as it relates to middle level curriculum has been reviewed. Several assumptions about the nature of educational change, as discussed in the literature, are framed in this chapter. In addition, middle school teachers have expressed their thoughts concerning curricular change. Their comments indicate that the change incurred during the planning and implementation of integrated or interdisciplinary projects was similar to what their colleagues experienced, yet unique in some ways. Certainly, the point of view of all participants in the change process is vital in understanding it as a complex whole. The voices of teachers are a critical link, for it is in the classrooms that curricular change takes place. As teachers' voices are validated in this process, so they are empowered to validate the voices of their students.

As a conclusion for this chapter, each of the assumptions about change is reconsidered with the imprint of middle school teachers' reflective comments. Categorizations of comments may reveal overlaps. Such overlaps support the notion that educational change, while it can be described in its various parts, is a complex whole.

CHANGE IS A HIGHLY PERSONAL EXPERIENCE.

- Get involved in curriculum integration in order to understand it.
- Be less bossy with team members.
- Work on oneself to develop a give and take attitude with teammates.
- Learn to trust oneself.
- Develop the role of partner with students.
- Make sacrifices.
- Be flexible.
- Endure frustrations.

The message here is that change is a personal experience because it requires each of us to give up control of others, to be willing to make sacrifices for the good of the group, and to endure frustrations along the way. Curriculum integration is worth far more than the struggles we encounter when working with others. Middle school teachers are well acquainted with the need for flexibility. It is the national password for entering a middle school! We, the community of middle school educators, require the most growth in learning to be in partnership with students in the learning environment. We cannot be successful until we abondon the "giver" of knowledge paradigm and become co-creators of curriculum with students.

CHANGE IS A PROCESS—IT TAKES TIME FOR CHANGE TO OCCUR.

- Give oneself time to fully explore curriculum integration.
- Allow the learning to create its own time frame.
- Gain confidence in the role of facilitator of learning.

- See students differently as they are empowered to have a say in their learning.

- Determine a starting place for your team, continue to grow, re-examine curriculum integration, reflect, improve.

- Learn to relax and allow learning to occur naturally.

- Leave behind the mold of "old, experienced" teachers vs. the "young, in-tune" teachers.

- Re-examine definitions of failure and success.

It is rare that people, when attempting to make changes in established practices, can immediately adopt a different set of behaviors. Learning to function as a facilitator of learning, allowing the learning to create its own time frame, and viewing students as creators of their own learning are behaviors that take time and endurance to internalize. We must give ourselves the freedom to work with change until it works with us!

CHANGE REQUIRES RISK TAKING BEFORE ALL THE DATA ARE IN!

- Enlist support from leadership in order to take risks.

- Teach outside your area of formal training.

- Empower students to create their own learning.

- Empower students by allowing them to determine how to demonstrate their learning.

- Let go of "the" curriculum.

- Risk being misunderstood by colleagues and central office personnel.

- Involve parents in the assessment of students' learning.

- Risk opening oneself for criticism.

- Learn to work together, even if your preference is to work alone.

- Allow one's professional vulnerabilities to be exposed.

- Get out of content "ruts."

- Get honest—reap comaraderie.

The risks might seem overwhelming for some, but teachers who philosophically support curriculum integration take risks in redefining the curriculum to meet students in their world of questions and concerns. Teams that do not function cohesively limit the potential impact they have for positive, relevant learning experiences for their students. Yes, curriculum integration requires teachers to get out of their content "ruts" and become part of learning experiences that are greater than the sum of that which is currently taught in subject-centered curriculum. Two things teachers must do: let go and empower! Let go of *the* curriculum and empower students to be partners in the development of *their* curriculum.

CHANGE IS LEARNING, AND IT IS SURROUNDED WITH UNCERTAINTY.

- Desire to test new ideas, but tendency to hold onto old beliefs.
- Unsure about commitment of teammates to work as a cohesive group.
- Uncertain about how specialists fit into curriculum.
- Uncertain about letting go of district curriculum.
- Uncertain about the variety of unknowns in any change effort.

Uncertainties are embedded in all changes. What we are faced with in dealing with uncertainty is the development of a plan that works, not only for us, but for our teammates, and ultimately our students. The unknowns regarding commitment of teammates in a change effort, the unknowns that threaten our security when asked to teach in areas outside our formal training, are important issues. The best plan, though, is to talk about these things. Get them on the table! That in itself may produce some anxiety, and certainly a level of trust must be established before such discussions can take place. It is a well-known fact that many of our fears or uncertainties are lessened by getting them out in the open. Discussed in an atmosphere of trust and support, uncertainties lose their power over us.

REFERENCES

Beane, J. (1993). *A middle school curriculum: From rhetoric to reality* (2nd ed.). Columbus, OH: National Middle School Association.

Dewey, J. (1915). *The school and society* (rev. ed.). Chicago: University of Chicago Press.

Eson, M. E., & Wolmsky, S. A. (1980). Promoting cognitive and psycholinguistic development. In Johnson, J. (Ed.), *Toward adolescence: The middle school years, 79th yearbook of the National Society for the Study of Education: Part one.* Chicago: The University of Chicago Press.

Fullan, M. (1991). *The new meaning of educational change.* Columbia: Teachers College Press.

Fullan, J., & Miles, J. (1992). Getting reform right: What works and what doesn't. *Phi Delta Kappan, 73* (10), 744–752.

Fuller, F. (1969). Concerns of teachers: A developmental conceptualization. *American Education Research Journal, 6* (2), 207–226.

Hall G., & Hord, S. (1984). *Change in schools: Facilitating the process.* New York: SUNY Press.

Nias, J., Southworth, G., & Yeomans, R. (1989). *Staff relationships in the primary school. A study of organizational cultures.* London: Cassell.

Phillips, J. (1981). *Piaget's theory: A primer.* San Francisco, CA: W.H. Freeman and Co.

CHAPTER 5

The Human Element: Teaming

Timothy Hillmer

It was February, the Colorado snow still heavy on the school grounds, when my teaching career changed. February, the month of "cabin fever," when a wild streak seemed to settle in over students as the halls got crazy and the winter rolled by. The weather outside seemed to match my mood— gray and overcast. A dark front moved in over the foothills to the west bringing more snow.

I was sitting outside my principal's office with a legal pad in my hands and four pages of hastily scribbled notes which contained ideas for a new integrated program at the middle level. I was preparing to go in and play educational poker. The stakes were high. I felt that my teaching ideals, hopes, and reputation were on the line. I was also aware that a lot of dreams could die in the next 30 minutes.

For the past year I had been working in an alternative program. The experience was a hard one, and in the months before Christmas I had watched our teaching team gradually splinter apart due to personality clashes, burnout, and philosophical differences. Our team planning sessions were dominated by unanswered questions. Should we use a multi-age classroom model or a straight grade level model? Should we have a tradi- tional assessment format with letter grades and points or move towards a non-graded, portfolio-based assessment? Should we use a program model where one teacher works closely with a small group of students and teaches all subjects or a true team teaching approach where all the teachers share all the students and teach from their specific strengths?

The team was currently in shambles. Our team leader had announced earlier in the week that he had accepted another job in Wyoming and would be leaving in March. Another member of the team had decided to finish the semester and then take a year off from education. My teaching partner and friend, frustrated and angry at not being listened to by the team, had already requested a transfer to the ninth grade.

The night before the meeting with my principal, I'd talked with my wife about whether to stay with the program and take a leadership role in rebuilding the team or seek another job at a local junior high school where I had previously taught. The first opportunity offered risk and excitement; the second, safety and security.

At one point my wife asked, "How will you feel if you try to rebuild the team and fail?" Puzzled, I thought for a few seconds, and then said, "That at least I tried." "And how will you feel if you don't try at all?" she asked. "Like I didn't even give it a chance," I said.

Later that night I thought of the students and parents who had already committed to the program and wondered if I would have the energy and time required for the responsibilities of being team leader: evening meetings with parents; after school and weekend planning sessions with the team; administrative decisions over how students are interviewed and selected for the program; and hours of time for orientation of new teachers. As the last existing team member who had not made a decision about the following year, I was aware that my principal would shut the program down if I left. He was not willing to start over from scratch. Was I leading the parents and students on by promising something unrealistic, something I could not deliver? Was false hope more cruel than no hope at all? *Why is teaming so important to me?* I thought. *Wouldn't it be easier to just go back to the junior high school and work alone?*

Learning about the Value of Teaming

For the first five years of my teaching career, I taught in a traditional junior high school setting with six classes a day of seventh grade language arts. Each class was 45 minutes long, and over the course of a single day I saw about 150 students. The school did not facilitate teaming, but instead teachers often worked in isolation. Because contact with other teachers was omitted, there were many school days when the only interactions I had with my colleagues were in the parking lot before and after school. The rare opportunities for communication with other teachers were usually in the faculty lounge over a 20 minute lunch, at department meetings, or at the in-services that took place every few months.

In my first and second years, even though I was cut off from other teachers, I enjoyed the sense of control I had over my classroom. It was as if I were the king of my own planet and no other ruler dared to step onto my turf. When the students came through the classroom door, they were stepping into my world of personally established rules and regulations.

The early years were definitely tough. I once had to deal with a challenging group of students who had plotted a revolution against me. I single-handedly squelched the ring-leaders by marching them down to the principal's office and arranging to have their parents notified about their imminent suspension. Months later I thought about that incident and shuddered with embarrassment. Not once did I even consider sitting down with my students and discussing the conflict or perhaps arranging a "cease fire" so that we could work out a treaty. I didn't have the skills to pull off such a thing, nor did I have a mentor or teammate to teach me the fine art of diplomatic negotiations.

This incident shook me up and showed me I needed the help and support of the other teachers. The feeling of control I'd once needed as a beginning teacher had been replaced by the sudden realization that I was shut in and cut off from interacting with the teachers down the hall. I did not like having to rely on my own limited ideas and skills to survive. Therefore, I started seeking out colleagues for new classroom management ideas, professional book suggestions, and creative lessons. Some shared with open arms; others guarded their classroom secrets as if they were gold. There were even a few instances when I collaborated with a teacher on a small lesson or unit or arranged to talk with another teacher after school about a new idea. I discovered that these brief interactions were energizing, almost "electric," and I began to suggest to the school administrators that we be given more time to plan and talk.

There was talk going around the building of moving to a true "middle school" model, where teachers were organized into teaching teams and given common planning time and a block of classrooms. Some teachers supported this idea. Of those who did, many were new to the profession and were struggling to gain tenure. On the other hand, most of the veteran teachers, who made up the majority of the staff, expressed that the schedule was fine and there wasn't any reason to "mess with a good thing." I speculated that they felt threatened by the idea of team organization because it meant opening up their classrooms to colleagues who might tamper with their "set in stone" curriculum. Some seemed nervous about the amount of time and extra work teaming would require. They appeared frightened by the idea of teaching out of their subject area and quoted research at faculty meetings that said an integrated curriculum would mean the death of the pure academic subjects.

By my fifth year, the administration had worked out a schedule that allowed for some common planning time, and for teachers to be assigned to teaching teams so they could discuss their students. Many of the veteran teachers scoffed at this change as another trend that would eventually pass.

Most of the teams continued to go about business as usual with their six individual classes and made little attempt to integrate curriculum. Team teaching seldom occurred. I remained locked in my tightly scheduled world, yearning for an opportunity to actually team with a group of colleagues who shared my vision of an integrated curriculum.

I left this school soon afterward when a wonderful opportunity came my way. I applied to be a Teacher on Special Assignment (TOSA) for the district and was assigned to help supervise and administer a new philosophy of curriculum and instruction that discouraged lectures and worksheets and encouraged an integrated curriculum and collaborative learning. For the next year and a half I traveled to all the middle and high schools to work with language arts teachers in their classrooms. It was a marvelous and challenging experience and gave me a chance to see first hand what was really going on in classrooms across the district.

While I observed some instances of effective teaming, the majority of teachers were working alone in their rooms and seemed nervous when I would ask to visit their classes. I began to see a pattern of disconnected, isolated teachers who had few interactions with their colleagues. I met teachers who felt just as cut off, just as stuck, and just as helpless as I had at my old school.

TEAMING "AIN'T" EASY

When I learned I would be going back into the classroom again, I knew I wanted something different. I wanted to be part of a teaching team, and I was determined to find one. This was not an easy task, however. While I was a TOSA, I had witnessed few good examples of effective teaming, though I learned that many of the middle school teachers expressed a willingness to try teaming, if given the opportunity.

Then I discovered an alternative program for sixth, seventh, and eighth graders that had been created by teachers, parents, and administrators as a "bridge" between the existing alternative elementary school and the more traditional high school setting. This alternative program for young adolescents was a "school within a school" and housed within a functioning junior high school. It offered multi-grade level classrooms, team teaching opportunities, and an emphasis on experiential learning. I applied for a vacancy on the team and was soon hired. I was excited to have the opportunity to collaborate with three other teachers, and to be a part of a team.

Our administrators were supportive and gave the team tremendous flexibility and freedom when it came to scheduling, curriculum implementation, evaluation, experiential learning, and other innovative concepts. Our classrooms were all within close proximity and we had a large space with breakdown walls for whole program activities.

I was ecstatic about my new teaching situation. At the time it seemed like the perfect scenario, an oasis within the educational desert. I met all the other members of the teaching team in the interview and they seemed warm and very professional. One of them was also new to the program, and she seemed thrilled about the wonderful possibilities of four experienced teachers working as a team.

Within a few weeks of the beginning of school, however, I knew there were problems. The main problem became apparent during our team meetings in the way we communicated. The meetings were often unstructured, with no agenda. Conversations would erupt about students, parents, or the current problems that needed to be solved. Consequently, team meetings were spent putting out "fires," and never addressing long-term goals or how we functioned as a team. Norms were never established because there seemed to be an underlying assumption that everyone already knew and understood how to operate as a team.

I also came to realize that some of my original ideas about the program had been wrong. I'd been led to believe that all the classrooms would be mixed grade level, when in fact the grade levels were kept very separate. The only time they blended was during special "mini-courses," which lasted a week and occurred once every few months. I also expected that since we would be team teaching with teachers who had expertise in social studies and science, I did not need to worry about my lack of expertise in these two subjects.

The fall and early winter left me feeling overwhelmed and confused. The work load was tremendous, and, for the first time, I found myself teaching science and social studies and health, as well as a ninth grade language arts class outside of the program. I was paired up with the other newcomer to the team and assigned to work with thirty-five 7th graders. We received very little assistance from the two veteran teachers on the team. In fact, except for team meetings, I rarely had contact with them.

I soon came to realize that they were both still recovering from the previous year, when they had worked with two difficult teachers who eventually left the school, and when they had been assigned an extremely challenging group of students, with a demanding parent population. They were "burned out," content to take their respective sixth and eighth grade students and retreat to their own classrooms. Occasionally, they would help us with individual lessons, but they didn't have the energy or the initiative to really provide any guidance. So my teammate and I were left stranded with the seventh graders and without the knowledge or experience necessary to integrate science or social studies with the language arts curriculum. I felt abandoned by the team.

Looking back on this situation, I now realize that I did not handle it very well. Since I was new to the team, I did not want to step on anyone's toes or offend the other two teachers who had developed the program. So I remained silent and worked hard and did whatever the team required. I waited for someone on the team to ask me how things were going or to invite me to share my opinion. The invitation never came. The ensuing months were the hardest of my teaching career. For the most part, I enjoyed working with the students, but the team situation was crippling me each day. When February arrived and things just seemed to be getting worse, I thought a great deal about returning to my old junior high classroom, where I had worked alone and been in charge. The alternative program I once thought would be an oasis for me had somehow turned into a mirage that promised the illusion of water, but presented only dry sand.

When I left my principal's office that February afternoon I was thrilled. He had been tremendously supportive of the ideas I had presented, everything from alternative assessment without letter grades to multi-grade-level classrooms to teaching physical education within the program. He wanted this alternative program to continue and felt relieved that I was willing to take on a leadership role in its development. He also agreed that I needed to play a major role in the selection process for the new teachers. I left the office floating with excitement about the possibilities for the following year.

First, I needed to find the right people for the team. I'd learned the hard way that the most important resources of a solid team are the people themselves. So I began making phone calls to former colleagues in other buildings and putting the word out about what we were going to try the following year. Most importantly, I contacted some teachers with whom I had become acquainted through professional organizations or with whom I had previously worked.

The next few months were a whirlwind of activity, along with my regular teaching duties. When the day finally arrived for the teacher interviews, I was amazed at the quality of the candidates. One parent who sat in on the interview panel said that it was the most impressive line-up of teachers she had ever seen. One thing was consistent about all the candidates. Many of them were teaching in situations where they had little interactions with their colleagues and hardly any chance to plan or team teach, and they were hungry for the opportunities that this alternative program presented. In the end, the panel (comprised of administrators, parents, students, and myself) selected three solid teachers known for their professionalism, creativity, energy, and positive interactions with students. This new team would end up working together for the next three years.

Learning about Teaming: The Power and the Perils

If any of us had known what lay ahead, there is a good chance we might have pursued other career options. The events that followed were an odd and sometimes unsettling mix of failures, triumphs, confrontations, celebrations, and startling revelations. We dealt with a minority group of angry parents and students who were so upset about the changes we had implemented in the program that they tried to intimidate and manipulate us by spreading false rumors, questioning our professional judgment, and threatening to pull their children out of the program. We clashed with other teachers in the traditional junior high school who felt that our alternative approach to education was not "academically rigorous" enough to meet the school's standards. We tried thematic units in an attempt to connect the disciplines and discovered how enormously complex it was to fully integrate multi-grade-level classrooms. We went on numerous field trips that tested our patience and endurance and commitment to the program and the students. But the hardest obstacle of all was when we fought among ourselves.

During those three years we all dealt with personal problems that required each other's support, flexibility, and understanding. Despite these numerous problems, we felt this alternative program still contained a great deal of promise. So, we expanded the program in our second year and hired a new teacher.

Even though we were committed and believed in the value of teaming, we disagreed about such things as:

- standards of discipline and consequences
- authentic assessment of student work
- internal decisions about how to handle conflicts with team members
- field trip planning
- parental concerns
- how to integrate, given the curriculum guidelines mandated by

the district

- creating an effective yet flexible schedule
- how to divide up teaching assignments and duties

Amazingly, three years passed, and the core of our team remained together. Our program grew from 70 to 125 students. We also added one more teacher who fit in beautifully with the direction and philosophy of our program.

Each day I am impressed and proud that we are still together as a team. Upon reflection, I realize that we made some mistakes along the way. We also made some incredibly wise decisions about how to operate as a teaching unit. I do not think I fully realized how fortunate our team was until I attended a recent in-service that was held by my school district.

The presenter was a nationally known consultant who had been invited to speak with us about our recent transition from traditional junior high schools to middle schools. At one point in the presentation, she asked us to walk around the room and talk with a variety of teachers from other buildings and other teams about integrated curriculum. I spent 20 minutes at the task, but discovered that not once did I talk about the recommended subject. Each time I began conversations with other teachers and asked how things were going, their responses were almost identical: "Well, the teachers on our team just don't get along, so we're not doing much teaming"; or "I'm not even talking to my teammates anymore"; or "They're not supportive of my classroom management style, so I just do my own thing and they leave me alone."

Their responses didn't surprise me. Within my own building, which had recently made the switch to middle schools, I knew grade-level teams were beginning to fragment. I had watched a six-person team quickly break down to three 2 person teams due to professional and personal conflicts. One eighth grade team refused to integrate by choosing to remain secluded in their classrooms in order to teach the same traditional content areas they had always taught in the junior high school.

THE HUMAN ELEMENT OF TEAMING

Why is teaming so hard? This question has haunted me for five years. I believe the answer lies in the "human element" of the team, an area that is often overlooked. The human element presents an entirely different set of problems from scheduling, assessment, and integration. Just because administrators occasionally give teachers some team building inservice time as well as some choice with whom they might like to work, it does not guarantee "happy teams working in harmony."

I am not suggesting "team therapy," although there may be times when confronting team issues and problems could feel like a therapy session. Some individuals might be uncomfortable with what I'm suggesting, but I feel so strongly about this issue that I think it's worth a little discomfort to prevent a team from internal self-destruction.

DEALING WITH FEAR, DISTRUST, AND ANXIETY

Even though I entered that rebuilding year with a moderate amount of conflict resolution skills which I'd learned as a TOSA, I hardly ever used them. Instead I relied on a very different model of team building that I'd picked up during my ten seasons as a whitewater rafting guide on rivers throughout the western United States. I felt I needed to look at the new team not from the perspective of a teacher, but from the point of view of a river guide.

Many of our raft trips were one to two days in length, which meant that I had a relatively short amount of time to take five to seven inexperienced tourists and somehow transform them into a single paddling unit. They needed to be able to negotiate a series of difficult and sometimes treacherous obstacles on the river and also deal with emergency situations. All of this had to be understood and agreed upon before the first wave broke across the bow of the raft.

As a guide, my formula was simple. I understood that before I could ever hope to build a team in such a short amount of time, I first had to deal with the basic human elements that could easily undermine our goal: fear, distrust, and anxiety. I had witnessed too many experiences where these emotions surfaced halfway through a difficult trip, only to undermine my leadership and divide the crew.

In many ways the teachers who were going to work together in this alternative program were like a new rafting team—we were all in the same boat preparing for a difficult challenge that would require us to work together. Our professional lives depended on it. And before we could launch into the perilous currents that awaited us, we first had to address the human elements that could either help a team work together or smash them into pieces. Not only did we need to learn how to be in the same boat, but we also had to figure out how to paddle it.

So I set aside time at our initial meetings to first talk about some of our own fears and anxieties as we headed into the year. We talked about past experiences in our teaching careers that had been frustrating and sometimes frightening. We talked about our "best case scenarios" for the year, as well as our "worst." We talked about our strengths and weaknesses as educators and those particular issues or situations that had often gotten us into trouble. As the team leader, I tried to stress again and again how important it was that this alternative program needed to be a healthy place to work, and that the top priority had to be taking care of ourselves as individuals both at school and at home. What good is a program without teachers? If we burn out like the last team and end up leaving, the kids and parents who committed to this alternative program will be left with nothing. The teachers are the heart and soul of this program, and we have to work together to create a place we enjoy and respect.

Like river rafting, a guide or team leader needs to deal with the other issues concerning the health and emotional well-being of the team, such as fear, anxiety, assigning roles, establishing norms and expectations, and helping to regroup when things get crazy or out of control. The leader should have his/her finger on the "human element" and "communication" pulse of the team throughout the year and be a leader in this area. S(he) should not have to deal with team finances, textbook selections, and district curriculum responsibilities. These management and organizational tasks should be spread out among the other team members so that *everyone's* talents are used and the work load is divided as equitably as possible.

Trust is essential. Developing trust among team members is something that takes time and cannot be expected to happen overnight. Team members need to have numerous opportunities every month to "check in" with each other and talk about how things are going from their perspective. Team norms need to be clearly established so that conflicts/disagreements/misunderstandings can be dealt with as soon as possible through mediation and direct conversation among the team members involved. Sensitivity, honesty, and respect are key words when dealing with conflict. If teachers can listen and be sensitive to each other's perspective, as well as be honest about their own feelings, then there is a strong chance that each team member will feel respect and trust for his or her colleagues, as well as feel respected and trusted himself or herself.

10 Steps Toward Team Building

Building a cohesive teaching team is a complicated and difficult task. There are many aspects regarding the human element which need to be addressed if teachers hope to work synergistically together to integrate curriculum. Here are some procedures which I have learned that foster team building:

1) *If possible, arrange with your administrators to have some paid time before the school year begins to meet / plan / get to know each other.*

   This step is often left out due to time and money constraints and scheduling pressure. Try to do it before the "hustle" of school begins and arrange to bring in someone from the outside (a facilitator or school counselor) to lead the meeting/retreat. Perhaps the get-together could be tied in with something fun that all team members enjoy, whether it be cooking a meal together or going for a hike. (This year our team is planning a rafting trip for the staff in order to reflect upon our successes and failures.) The length of this meeting/retreat is up to the team. What's essential is that at some point the team has a chance to share their hopes, dreams, and fears for the coming school year. Some good questions to ask of team members might be:

   - What's the best thing that could happen this year with our team?
   - What's the worst thing?
   - What are your hopes as we head into the year?
   - What are your fears?
   - What are our strengths as a team?
   - What might our weaknesses be?

2) *Make it a priority at the beginning of the year to have social gatherings.* Social time should not be discounted as something unnecessary or trivial. It's an essential aspect of building community. Unfortunately, when a team is under a great deal of stress, it is often the first thing to be eliminated. Social gatherings provide an opportunity to get to know the other members of the team in a low-stress, non-threatening environment. It's also a chance to meet their families and friends and begin to understand what their lives are like outside of school. Establish firm dates for these gatherings and mark them on the team calendar. You may even want to appoint a team member to be in charge of social events. His or her task might be to remind the team that these events are important to the health and dynamics of the team. Our team established a monthly F.A.C. (Friday Afternoon Club) after school when we would gather at a local restaurant to talk. If there's a team member who has a variety of after school commitments (child care, other employment, etc.), then perhaps

the team could be flexible and work out a way to help this person attend.

3) *In the beginning establish some "norms" or team operating policies.* Don't assume that everyone on the team operates by the same set of rules. Norms basically address the issue of, "What is okay/what isn't okay?" For example, one norm that our team established is, "Go straight to the source if you have a problem or conflict with someone else." If a teacher is having a problem with a teammate, then s(he) should privately discuss this issue with that person as soon as possible. If the teacher doesn't feel comfortable talking with the other teacher by himself, then s(he) might enlist a team member to serve as mediator. The same policy/norm applies if an angry parent calls a teacher up on the phone and begins to complain about a colleague on the team. This parent should be told immediately to "go straight to the source" and talk with the teacher involved. It is not okay to take an indirect route when it comes to communication. If you can't say it to the person's face, then perhaps it shouldn't be said at all.

At the beginning of the last school year, we generated a list of "community expectations" for our program that applied to both teachers and students:

- Teachers, students, and parents will share the decision-making process as much as possible.
- Be respectful of students, adults, and all school property.
- Try to be creative and flexible when solving problems.
- Participation is expected.
- Cooperate and communicate with others.
- Be on time for classes and special meetings.
- Start and end class on time.
- Be organized and work to the best of your ability.
- Be responsible for your own actions and words.
- Go straight to the source if you have a problem/conflict with a teacher/student.

4) *Establish a weekly or monthly team meeting for "emotional check in" with each other.* Nothing else should be included on the team agenda. Our team has a "feelings" session every Friday. Again, this may sound like a therapy session, but it has become the

single most important component of our team meetings. Without this 40 minutes a week, none of the other plans or activities or integrated units we discuss would be possible. It helps to "clear the air" and keep us working together as a healthy unit. You may want to invite one of the school counselors /administrators to facilitate this session. The idea is simple: teachers go around the room and talk about how things have been going for them both personally and professionally. Each teacher gets an opportunity to speak. Issues that are brought up in the room need to stay in the room and be considered "privileged information." Sometimes a teacher may talk about a team-related issue that has bothered him or made him frustrated or angry. Another teacher may want to celebrate with the team something wonderful that has happened in the classroom. This can also be the place where teachers can bring up personal conflicts /successes that have been going on in their lives. Teachers should never be pressured to talk about home/family issues that they are not comfortable discussing. However, it needs to be made clear that if an individual is having a personal conflict/crisis in his or her life outside of school, there is a good chance that this issue will carry over into his or her professional life as well.

For example, last fall I had a very close friend in another city who was suddenly diagnosed with cancer. His condition rapidly deteriorated and he died before Thanksgiving. It was an agonizing and painful time for me, and I knew it was affecting the quality of my teaching as well as my ability to "carry the load" on the team. So I made sure my colleagues were aware of the situation. This was not used as an excuse in any way. I felt that my teammates needed to know what I was going through so there wouldn't be any misunderstandings or wrong assumptions made, and I trusted them with this personal information.

Time and again I've seen how important this component is. If teachers do not have a regular forum to talk about their own feelings, conflicts, and stress-related issues, then it is highly possible that a teammate could make an invalid assumption about the attitude/behavior of a colleague, which could then lead to a misunderstanding. As team members who are involved in a learning community, we need to constantly remind ourselves that our number one goal should be to model healthy behaviors for our students.

5) *Be aware of each other's strengths and make them the foundation of the team.* At the beginning of the year, have each team member write down what strengths s(he) is bringing to the group. These should include skills/hobbies/activities in which they have some expertise or background as well as academic strengths. Once this pool of resources is established, the team can begin planning for the year.

In our alternative program, the team is constantly utilizing our "talent bank" when we organize field trips, enrichment days, mini-courses, and integrated units. We just completed a successful "mini-society" unit where we studied economics. Instead of having each teacher use the same curriculum and teach it the same way to all of our students, we let each teacher offer a different class based on their own expertise or interest in this area, then let the students choose from a multitude of selections. In other words, each of us chose to teach economics by viewing it through a different "lens" based on our own interests. This kind of approach allowed our middle level students the opportunity to also view economics through different lenses.

One teacher with a strong background in computers and ham radio operations chose to look at economics from a technological perspective. Another teacher who had an interest in the stock exchange taught his economics unit from the perspective of the stock market and how it affects the economy. I chose to offer the "economics of the performing arts," where students visited a wide variety of theater companies, interviewed and listened to a multitude of performing artists, and created their own "mini-theater" companies in order to understand the realities of what it meant to survive in today's economy as a performing artist. This unit could never have had such a rich flavor and variety for the students unless the team had worked from its strengths when we were in the planning stages. I think that far too often teams plan projects and units based on their limitations rather than on their strengths.

6) *Respect each individual teacher's classroom expectations and academic standards and be sensitive when asking teachers to make changes.* Teaming, to whatever degree, often requires a teacher to make sacrifices or changes for the benefit of the program. If teachers are asked to make a somewhat radical change in their student/classroom expectations, or in their

academic standards, they may feel a great deal of professional resentment towards the team if the issue is not handled in a sensitive manner.

Teachers often have a passion for a particular subject area, whether it be reading, writing, science, geography, history, math, or a foreign language. In many ways they might feel that this subject is essential to a student's education and that it must be taught in a certain way and cover a certain amount of information in order to have the proper impact on students. When teachers are asked to sacrifice or make changes that affect what and how they teach, they may feel threatened or devalued. This very human reaction might be followed by resistance or even retaliation in order to hold their ground.

When a team of teachers is split over student expectations regarding homework, behavior, or academic standards, the split can be further widened if a compromise or "middle ground" isn't reached. It has been my past experience that often this issue is not acknowledged directly in a team meeting, but instead left to simmer and then boil over at a later time. The results can be disastrous and divisive. The team leader should schedule an entire meeting to resolve this issue, perhaps with the assistance of a school counselor or a neutral party as facilitator.

This is a potentially volatile issue. If teachers are forced to change their classroom practices or expectations, they may feel unwilling to compromise and might harbor resentment at not being heard or respected. It is vital that each member of the team be given the chance to express his or her opinion. It is also important that once a decision has been made, it is one that everyone on the team can live with, no matter what the consequences.

This type of conflict resolution requires a great deal of skill. I strongly suggest that an "experienced outsider" be brought in to help the team work through this. Whether it be an administrator or a counselor, the issue is often too "hot" for the team leader to handle. It must also be made clear to the team beforehand that there are no perfect solutions. Part of successful teaming is the realization that team members do not always get what they want, and sometimes sacrifices have to be made.

7) *Try to share as much of the team responsibilities as possible.* Once

again, try to work from your strengths in this area. Take a look at all the different tasks, responsibilities, and jobs that the team has to manage. Then ask each team member to either write down or talk about where they feel their strengths are in these areas. If a teacher has an especially strong relationship with students, then s(he) might be asked to be the student liaison. If there is a teacher who has administrative aspirations, then s(he) might be asked to work closely with building administrators. Each team will be different in the way it splits responsibilities. The most important thing is that the jobs are shared and not simply "piled" on the team leader. All members of the team will have their roles and be expected to fulfill their responsibilities.

8) *Have some type of agenda for the team meeting and keep an agenda book with notes of the meetings.* Because time is so limited within a school schedule, it is essential that teams have an agenda for their meetings. The agenda can be formal or informal, tightly structured or very flexible. Each team will be different. Regardless, it's important that each meeting have an agenda and that some kind of record be kept of what was covered at the meeting. If teachers are absent, they can look back over the agenda and get a general idea of what was discussed. This book should be centrally located so that teachers can add items to future meetings and thus develop the agendas.

9) *The team should try to have a weekly schedule for their team meetings.* If there are certain issues that need to be dealt with each week, then plan to designate certain days to address these topics. For example, every Wednesday will focus on student issues. Another day could be designated for interpersonal team issues. Another day might be an opportunity to check in with a building administrator regarding school-wide issues. If some type of schedule is not in place at the beginning of the year, the team meetings could become "gripe sessions" where the same issues are dealt with repeatedly, or perhaps a place to put out the most current "fire." Just as students need a certain amount of consistency in their school and classroom schedules, so teams require a similar stability to have a healthy climate.

10) *Teams should be encouraged to develop their own unique look and style.* It would be a huge mistake to expect all teams to look the same. Just as writers are encouraged to develop their own voice, teams should be encouraged to create what works for

them. Some teams face a great number of limitations when they begin: huge classes; small classroom facilities; inflexible blocks of time. With those obstacles confronting a team, it is very difficult to work together effectively. It might be more realistic to see the team as more of a planning/communication unit that will successfully and consistently coordinate an educational program for a group of students. However, once a team is able to reduce the number of students in each class, utilize a large classroom space, and work out a block schedule, the teachers should be able to collaborate in a variety of ways.

Teaming: A Model for Our Students

Teaming can be a perilous endeavor when the basic human elements and needs of each team are not addressed. If the team is not able to talk in a consistently open and honest way about their fears, hopes, and conflicts, it may only reach a surface level of operation. Eventually, however, this seemingly calm exterior will begin to ripple and crack from the issues hidden under the surface. Whether students will admit it or not, they look to their teachers for guidance and leadership. When they see a group of adults operating in a manipulative, antagonistic, and untrusting manner, they might assume that this is the standard way to behave in a group. It is up to the teaching team to demonstrate a better and healthier way to interact with one another.

Teaming in the middle school can be an incredibly powerful force in educating students. When a team of teachers pool their strengths, resources, insights, past histories, and disciplinary skills, they can create almost anything. When the team models the attributes of cooperation, communication, trust, respect, support, and understanding for one another, they're also modeling the habits that students will need to carry with them in order to work successfully in the adult world.

CHAPTER 6

Thinking, Wondering, and Imagining: An Authentic Research Process in Action

Janice V. Kristo and Betty Robinson

> *"Is it research today?" T.J. asked as he hurriedly raced to my desk.*
>
> *"That's correct!" I responded.*
>
> *"YES!!" replied T.J., using a hand gesture to give extra emphasis to "YES!" Then he quickly turned and ran to his research folder to gather his materials and books for the next eighty minute period.*
>
> *T.J.'s comment is a typical one that I hear during our research unit. It sometimes amazes me that kids can look at this time block with such excitement. After all, research is hard work! It's like a giant puzzle with lots of pieces that over time interlock and connect to finally become a finished product.*
>
> *- Betty Robinson, sixth grade teacher*

Betty Robinson, a sixth grade language arts teacher, and Jan Kristo, a university faculty member, work as co-investigators to explore how the processes of inquiry and research writing evolve in Betty's classroom.

Research is both a challenging *and* rewarding process for Betty's students. They leave sixth grade with the tools and resources to continue a process of inquiry for a lifetime of learning. Actually we prefer to use Martinello and Cook's term (1994) "habits of mind" in reference to the development of tools, resources, and skills. Betty enables students to identify questions and then helps them satisfy their curiosities through a research process.

As long as we are alive there are questions to be asked, lessons to be learned, and new inquiries to be made. As educators we are curious about the process learners go through to make new discoveries. Children and young adults have a natural curiosity about life that begins at birth; the world around them is interesting and new. They ask questions and seek information to satisfy their curiosities. If the conditions in school are such that children and young adults are invited to pursue their inquiries, they won't abandon this desire to learn.

It is up to teachers then to further develop these tools and introduce students to the unlimited resources available which can be used to pursue answers to their questions. Watson, Burke, and Harste (1989) state that, "Inquiry is natural to all of us as learners" (p. 26). At the same time, we are interested in helping students make decisions and choices about their learning, as well as developing their own unique researcher's voice (using the voice of nonfiction writing) through a process of developing questions and pursuing answers through reading, writing, listening, and speaking.

The research process in this classroom demonstrates not only an integration of the language arts, but an integration of curriculum. At first Betty's students react somewhat puzzled when she says that they may pursue any topic they wish. For instance, Niki pipes up and says, "Well, I wanted to learn more about the brain, but that's a science topic!" Jeffrey exclaims, "I'm interested in finding out about the first people to ever settle in Maine. Isn't that more history and not English. Isn't this an English Class?" These questions presented a great teachable moment for Betty. She had no idea that kids would ask such questions, but she quickly realized how students perceive the curriculum—like a pie divided into little pieces. And why shouldn't students view their learning in this way? After all, their instructional history has separated all areas of study. Tchudi (1991) states that, "Teaching more history, ironically and perhaps predictably, won't result in learning more history. Pushing more disciplinary science won't necessarily produce children who know about science; in fact it may even create children who simply don't like science. And one has only to look at mathematics and its headlines to see what teaching a discipline in isolation will do" (p. 14).

Betty took the opportunity to talk with students about how the language arts—reading, writing, listening, and speaking—cut across the curriculum. English is not a subject, but gives students the tools or habits of mind to explore many disciplines—topics in math, science, social studies, and the arts, etc. In fact, as they pursue their research projects, she told them how they would discuss the ways the curriculum—all that they study—is connected. Their research projects would help them think in bigger ways about their own learning process and begin to discover links between their course work in individual subjects. This all seemed a little foreign to students, but they have begun to expect the unexpected from Betty, and they trust her when she says, "Be patient; things will emerge!"

Do you remember learning a research process in school? Unfortunately, our memories are filled with writing reports in social studies and science in junior high many years ago, but not quite knowing how to go about the task. We looked up all the information we could find about fossils, the Civil War, or whatever, in the encyclopedia. We recall the encyclopedia being the only reference we searched for information on our topic. It became almost a "sacred" text—the source with all the information we could ever imagine using. Next, we cleverly attempted to paraphrase the information in the encyclopedia to write "the report." The best part was designing the cover of the report, putting forth our best effort to create a fancy and creative cover that would impress and amaze our teachers, because we knew the content of our report would be as boring as what we found in the encyclopedia! We had no questions about what we wanted to find out, and there was no such thing as a research process that helped us make judgments and discoveries.

As we reflected upon our own experiences, we wondered what we had learned, but more importantly, what we hadn't learned! We did not catch the spirit and joy of wondering and imagining in school. We reserved that kind of learning to what we explored, talked, and wrote about outside of school. And, unfortunately we didn't see that our writing was really an invention (Graves, 1989); it was simply copying or paraphrasing, at best, another's words.

This chapter will discuss the research process in Betty's classroom as a learning journey in which students discover new strategies about ways to make inquiries that are meaningful and relevant to them. Betty combines a process approach to writing, reader's workshop routines, and cooperative learning to facilitate a process for research. Students are guided in the use of multiple library resources ranging from *The Reader's Guide to Periodicals* and computer programs providing new informational sources to nonfiction and other genres. Betty works in close cooperation with the media specialist to develop activities that help students build a level of comfort and ease in using the library and all of its resources. Students also learn ways to share and celebrate their learning with the classroom community.

We will discuss the following steps of the research process in Betty's class.

Learning How to Do Research: Developing Habits of Mind
- Establishing Writer's Workshop
- Organizing cooperative and collaborative learning and research groups
- Brainstorming topics of interest

- Identifying research questions
- Showing rather than telling: becoming critical consumers of information
- Gathering resources
- Using the resources of the media center and other libraries
- Identifying pertinent information
- Recording pertinent information
- Organizing the bibliography
- Organizing research questions and writing leads to the research report
- Share circle
- Decisions about final products
- Celebrations

Establishing a Writer's Workshop

Students in Betty's eighty minute language arts classes are well versed in the routines of writer's workshop. They brainstorm ideas, free write, conference with each other, and revise and edit to develop fluent pieces of writing. Betty invites students to consider a variety of genres for their writing. She shares an abundance of high-quality literature—from nonfiction, fantasy, historical fiction, biography, and picture books, to poetry—to help link the work of published writers to classroom writers. Students also self-select from a wide variety of genres for their own personalized reading. So, it is not unusual for students in Betty's class to experiment with their writing to develop an array of pieces such as play scripts, poetry, operettas, musical lyrics, chapter books, adventure stories, and diaries of historical figures. Betty combines both the research process and the writing workshop to help students produce written pieces that look very different from the more traditional "written report." This research process is just one more avenue used to explore reading and writing in powerful ways.

Establishing a Spirit of Collaboration and Cooperation: Working and Learning with Each Other

Cooperative learning strategies are crucial to the research process. Watson, Burke, and Harste (1989) state, "The conventional view is that learning is a private, personal, and competitive process" (p. 24). Not so in Betty's classroom! Students will have at least six weeks of experiencing the writing process and cooperative learning strategies before they are asked to begin other aspects of the research process. Time is an important element. A good part of writer's workshop is devoted to reflecting and dialoguing about what is working, how the class is functioning as a learning community, and ways to improve as a community of readers and writers.

Johnson and Johnson (1994) developed a systematic way in which students can learn to work together to solve problems and develop the skills necessary to work in groups to learn new concepts and to complete tasks in all curricular areas. From the very beginning, students use these skills to help each other through steps of their research.

Usually, each cooperative learning team consists of four students, all working together to support and encourage each other's learning. The first teams are chosen by Betty so that the groups are heterogeneous. Other pairings might later be determined by topic interest or editing requirements, such as students grouped together who are best able to deal with the nitty-gritty of the final editing process.

In one class of 27 students, 13 were identified as children with special needs. These students were included in each of the cooperative learning teams. The teams learned to work together to create research questions, locate information, and provide feedback on each other's writing. Betty finds that the advice goes both ways. Many special-needs students have knowledge that can be used by their team members. For example, one morning, Todd rushed into the classroom at the beginning of the research block armed with books about Florida. These resources were not for his inquiry but for one of the members of his group. He remarked, "I was looking for books for my own research project, but I found these books for you on Florida. These are just what you need to answer those questions on favorite places to visit in Florida. I wrote a letter to my grandmother and told her about your project, and she sent me these books for you to use."

Guests in Betty's classroom often remark that they cannot tell the special-needs students from other students in the classroom. By observing the groups during their work periods, we are constantly amazed by the ways students use supportive language to move each other forward in their work. For example, Josh remarked, "Remember, Danny, when we helped each other find a new topic to write about in writing workshop? Well, I'm going to help you find some things to put on your web so that you can write a great research report. Don't worry, it's easy!"

From discussing how students go about helping each other, as well as learning from a variety of texts, they begin to see that writing, like the research process is, indeed, a social phenomenon (Christie, 1986). The success with which Betty's students work with each other is reflected in Galton and Williamson's (1992) statements:

> Finally the classroom ethos in which collaboration can flourish is one where there is consistency in the way in which teachers deal with issues related to classroom management and with matters relating to learning. Ways of working *with* groups as well as ways of learning *in* groups need to be the subject of negotiation between the teacher and the pupils. A powerful element in this negotiation process is the development of a shared understanding about the feelings generated by the requirement to collaborate with one's peers and an awareness that these feelings are responsible for certain kinds of behaviour when working in group settings (p. 144).

Brainstorming Topics to Research

Identifying personal topics of interest is a crucial step in the research process. The strategies for identifying areas of interest or questions facilitates decision-making. Students are now in a better position for identifying potential topics of interest. Think about how important these interest-generating strategies are for students. Try generating a list of potential topics yourself. Even as an adult this can be a difficult task, particularly if someone else, such as a teacher, has always identified those areas for you!

Betty is the quintessential model of a learner, a reader, and a writer—an adult who has many questions and wonderments about the world around her. She seizes every moment to demonstrate—**to show**—rather than to tell how she goes about every new strategy she wants students to learn.

At the beginning of the school year, Betty often shares an assortment of artifacts that represent her life—photos of when she was in sixth grade, her favorite poetry, photos of her husband and children, her hand-made quilts and baskets, and examples of her own writing. Betty invites students to take a look at these to help brainstorm what they can tell about her from the display. Then, she writes her name in the middle of the blackboard and asks students to help her create a web of her interests.

Betty invites students to sign-up as to when they would like to bring in objects from home which tell something about their lives, hobbies, interests, etc. It is a completely voluntary activity, and no student is pressured to participate. This is another example of a way to introduce students to the concept of both webbing and generating questions that emerge from interests.

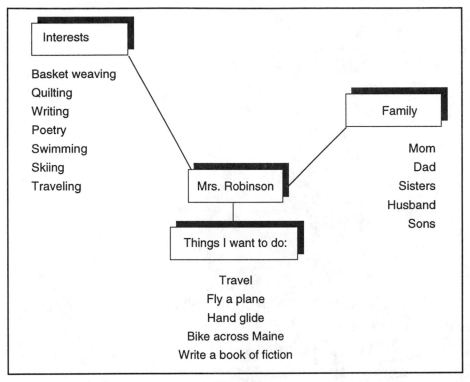

Figure 6.1
Mrs. Robinson's Web of Interests

Next, Betty asks students to brainstorm at least 25 topics they are curious about or want to explore. What do you wonder about as you walk or ride to school? What do you observe in your neighborhood? What is important to you? What do you take for granted? What do you wish for? What are your dreams? Betty finds Graves' book *Investigating Nonfiction* (1989) full of ideas for both her and her students to explore. With a little support and guidance, students generate their list with ease and lots of excitement. Several students note how similar this step is to brainstorming potential topics for the writer's workshop. When lists are completed, each student shares his or her list. As a result of this sharing, students often add new topics and/or questions to their own lists. It's not unusual for students to have over 100 items!

Nicolette's list included the following topics:

Topic List
Sea Otters
Jackie Robinson
Orca Whale
chimpanzees
Zebras
Diana Ross
Blacks/ Segregration
(Witches/Witch Craft)
Ghostes
Scoliosis
Cancer
Arthrites
North and South during Black segregration
Old Dolls
Mic Mac Indians
(Early Schools)
Robots
Loch Ness Monster (Nessie)
Africans
kangaroos
Phones
Manatee
Sugars
Aids
HIV
Human Body
Lois Lowery
Barbara Park
Jane Good all
Abe Lincoln

Figure 6.2

Each student selects a research partner to share the topic list and to receive feedback during all stages of the research process. They each have a research folder that contains a notebook, lists, webs, checklists, and other handouts. Next, students circle three topics that are of most interest and discuss why they chose these topics with their research partner. Sometimes students find that their partner is also interested in the topic or has information to share.

Identifying Research Questions

Finally, each student settles on one topic that will be the most interesting to research. The next step is designing a web with long spidery arms

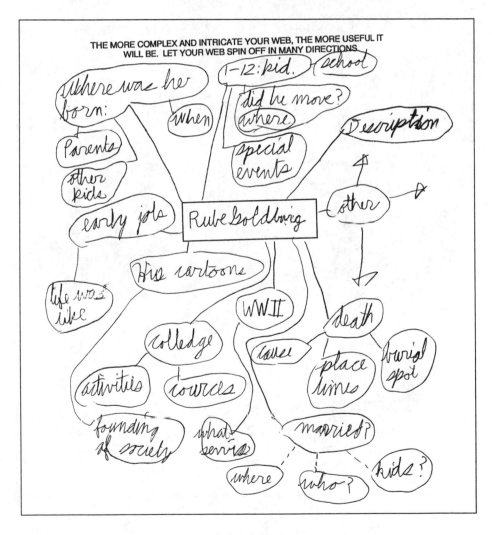

Figure 6.3

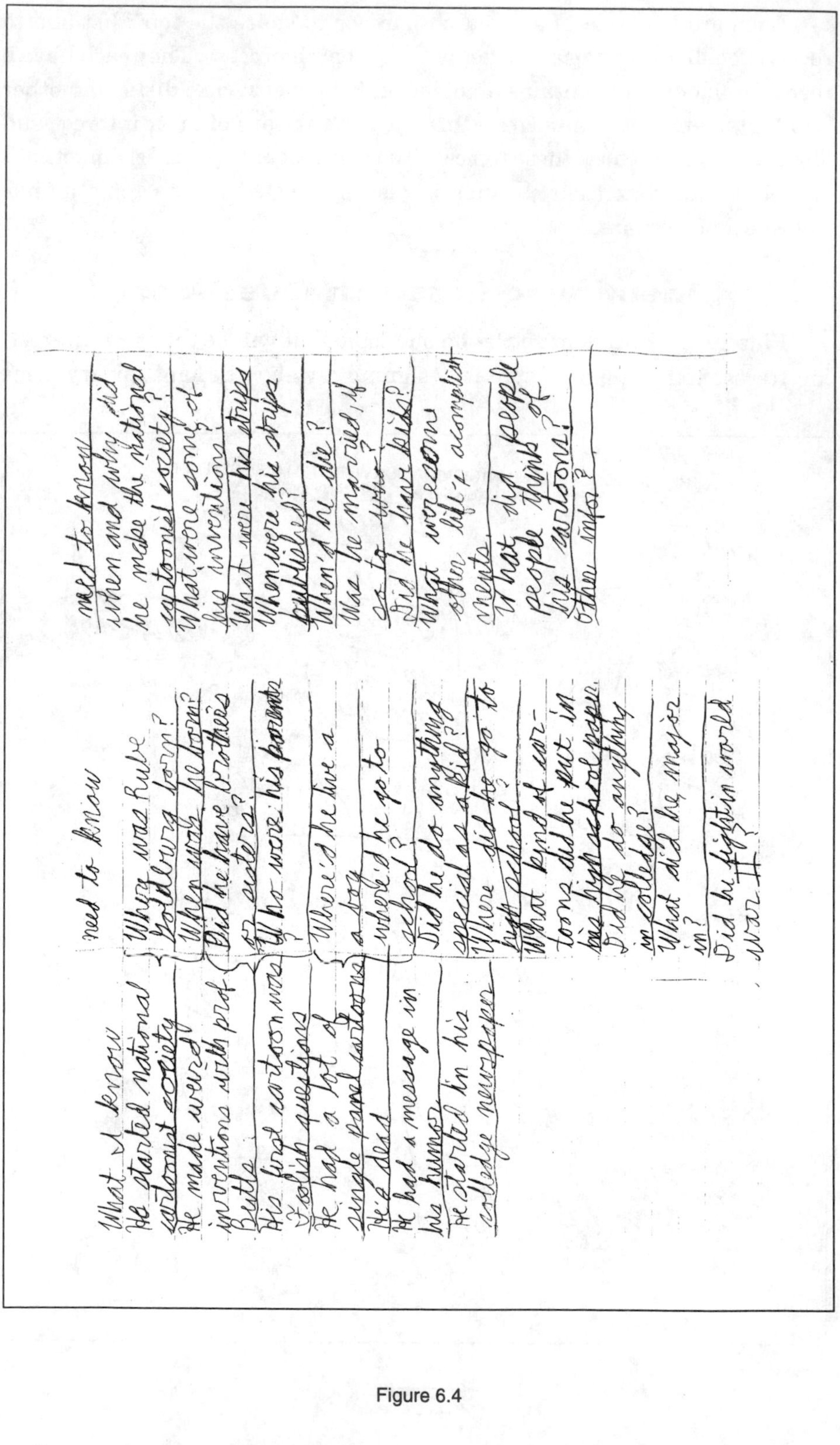

What I know
He started National Cartoonist Society
He made weird inventions with prof Butts
His first cartoon was of his questions
He had a lot of single panel cartoons
He's dead
He had a message in his humor
He started in his college newspaper

need to know
Where was Rube Goldberg born?
When was he born?
Did he have brothers + sisters?
Who were his parents?
Where'd he live as a kid?
Where'd he go to school?
Did he do anything special as a kid?
Where did he go to high school?
What kind of cartoons did he put in his high school paper?
Did he do anything in college?
What did he major in?
Did he fight in World War II?

need to know
When and why did he make the National Cartoonist Society?
What were some of his inventions?
What were his strips?
When were his strips published?
When'd he die?
Was he married? If so to who?
Did he have kids?
What were some other things he accomplished?
What did people think of his cartoons?
other inks?

Figure 6.4

extending from the topic. During another brainstorming session, Betty discusses the K-W-L strategy (Ogle, 1986)—What I KNOW about the topic, What I WANT to learn, and What I have LEARNED about the topic. Students first list things they already know and what they want to learn about the topic. Here is an example of Knud's web of inventor Rube Goldburg and lists of what he knows and wants to learn about the topic.

From Betty's experience, students have had little practice in identifying research questions. She finds that students need to practice writing their own questions and sharing these with research partners, as well as with her. From this sharing, discussion emerges concerning ways to narrow topics and to examine whether the research question(s) get to the "heart" of the inquiry. Betty's guidance and coaching are vital at this step of the process. Her goal is for students to be clear on what they want to research and what kinds of information they will need in order to pursue their inquiries. Students also use webbing to build a series of questions they want answered about the topic. By formulating specific questions about their topics, students can then learn to skim and scan a variety of materials, rather than working endlessly to learn everything about a topic. An example of Knud's questions and major research questions is depicted below.

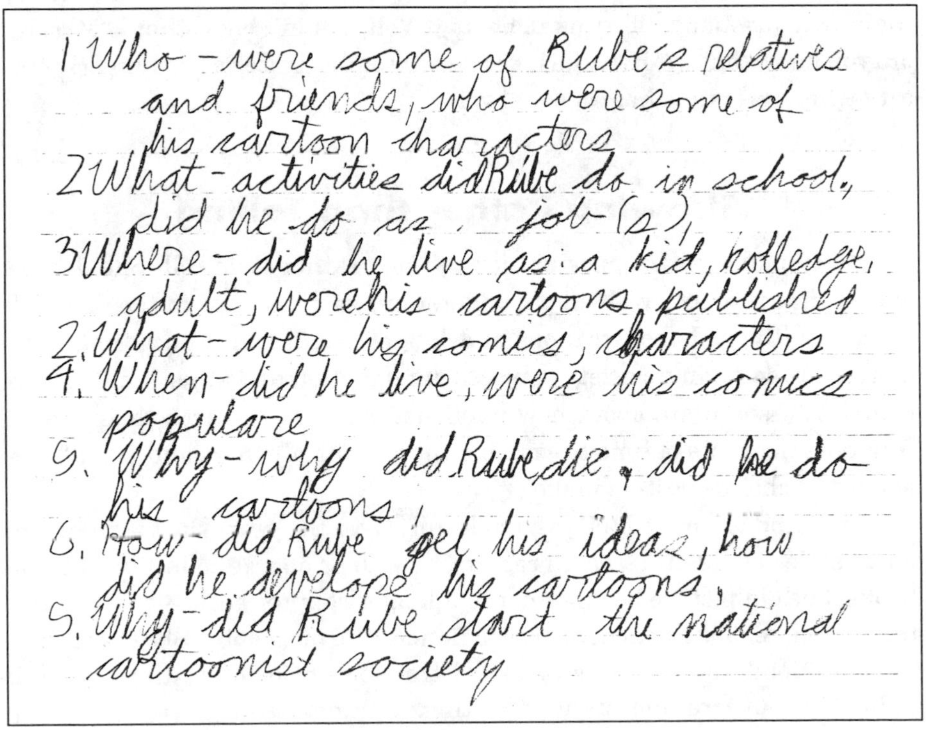

1 Who - were some of Rube's relatives and friends, who were some of his cartoon characters
2 What - activities did Rube do in school, did he do as a job (s),
3 Where - did he live as: a kid, kolledge, adult, were his cartoons published
2. What - were his comics, characters
4. When - did he live, were his comics populare
5. Why - why did Rube die, did he do his cartoons,
6. How - did Rube get his ideas, how did he develope his cartoons,
5. Why - did Rube start the national cartoonist society

Figure 6.5

MY MAJOR

RESEARCH QUESTION IS:

What did Rube Goldberg do in his lifetime?

Figure 6.6

Betty has observed repeatedly how students in one cooperative research team find leads to questions for students in their group as well as for other group members. Not only are students learning about their own topics, but they are learning about other topics, too. As students discover answers to their own questions, Betty often hears, "Well, I didn't know that!" "Mrs. R., did you know that...?" Betty has successfully orchestrated a learning community where everyone has an equal voice.

Showing Rather than Telling

Betty plans other opportunities to *show* rather than tell. She doesn't expect that students will simply understand various steps in the research process without demonstrations and lots of discussion. She literally immerses students in a variety of pieces of nonfiction and other materials as vehicles to speculate about how published authors research their topics. Students need lots of time to examine the writing of others and to dialogue about the choices writers make.

First and foremost, Betty is a collector! Over the years she has amassed a large file of student research reports, as well as a large collection of trade books, both in picture book format and longer chapter books—particularly nonfiction, realistic fiction, historical fiction, and biography. She shares this writing aloud and prepares overhead transparencies of writings by both published authors and student writing. Her next step is to try to help students get "inside of the writing." Much time is devoted to these explorations. Betty believes that students need to be literally "marinated" in different forms and styles of writing and to become conversant about them in order to be successful in writing their own pieces. Without this process of being "steeped" in literature, students left on their own will tend to rely on the most common text of nonfiction for their research—the encyclopedia. Because students read and talk about so many different forms of nonfiction writing, the encyclopedia only becomes *one* of many sources of information. It fades in comparison to the rich sources of writing Betty shares with students. She even shares and talks about her own nonfiction writing.

By sharing aloud the literature of published authors and the writing of previous students, Betty finds the following questions particularly helpful for students to consider in terms of what makes for interesting writing. She built this list over years of talking with students about their own writing during the research block. Betty samples from this list and uses the questions that make the most sense in terms of her observations of where students are with their own writing. Many questions are those that students actually formulated from their conversations about writing. Betty encourages students to continually add to and refine this list to make it "work" for them. Students find that many of these questions are helpful as they work and conference on their own pieces of writing.

Helpful Questions to Engage Dialogue about Writing

- As I share this piece aloud, do you find that you want to learn more? If so, why? What did the author do to make you want to keep on reading?

- What would you say about how the author developed the lead?

- What do you think about the author's choice of words?

- What would you say about the author's style of writing?

- In what ways does the author "break up" writing, such as the use of subtopics or subtitles, lists, borders around information, etc.?

- If the author uses dialogue, to what extent is it effective?

- What kinds of graphics are used throughout the writing— illustrations, tables, maps, photographs, timelines, charts, etc.?

- To what extent is this writing interesting to read? How is the writing "reader-friendly"?

- What do we know about the author's credentials for writing about this topic? Is a bibliography of sources included? What about a table of contents, glossary of terms, etc.?

- Is the writing done in a nontraditional format? Does the writing tell a story, while at the same time including facts or is the writing only factual? Does the author include poetry, diary or journal entries, humorous writing, etc.?

- What makes this reliable and convincing writing? To what extent is it persuasive? How can I tell what is fact and what is just the author's opinion?

- Who is the audience for this writing? Does the writing make any special demands on the reader? To what extent does the writer provide background information for the reader?

Alanna's Report on the Rain Forest

I think of a rain forest as a dark forest with,lots of trees,humidity , lots of rain, mist,animals ,insects, and dangling vines. I also think of it as a jungle. Jungle and rain forest mean the same thing [a thick tangled mass of tropical vegetation.]

There are four layers to a rain forest. The top layer is called the emergent layer. The trees are 115-150 feet tall. They can grow to 250 feet tall. That is as tall as a 25 story building. The canopy is below the emergent layer. The trees are 65 -100 feet tall. A plant named epiphytes depends on the trees there for support, also bromeliads grow on the trees too. They are related to pineapples. The understory is below the canopy. The understory doesn't get much sun because the canopy blocks out the sun. Next is the forest floor. The forest floor is filled with a lot of nutrients. There are a layer of rocks on the bottom with soil on the top.

In the rain forest there are a large variety of animals. I could never list them all but here are some . Katydid , leopard,muntjac[barking dear] , marmoset, piranha, lemur , sloth bear,spix macaw, kangaroo, squirrels, swallow,deer,owl monkey, cotton topped tamarin, snakes, colobus, iguana, bats, parrots, jaguar,gorillas,tigers, spider monkey , anteater, elephants,okapi,orangutans, gecko, golden lion tamarins, harpy eagle[the largest eagle in the world], bowerbird, toucan, alligator chameleon chimpanzees, gibbons [apes] golicith, hoatzin, and hummingbirds.

There are a lot of animals that are becoming extinct. Some are being killed by poachers like the gorilla. Poachers cut off there hands and heads. There hands are used for ashtrays. Golden Lion Tamarins are endangered to . They are orange animals and eat insects,lizards, and fruits. A lot of people capture the animals and keep them as pets. Almost all their homes have been destroyed because people are cutting down trees. Some other endangered animals are elephants, tigers, and orangutans.

Animals can communicate to show the way they are feeling. Animals use bright colors to attract attention to the opposite sex. Butterflies,moth's , and bugs camouflage themselves on one side of there wings to protect themselves from animals that might try to eat them. Animals protect their territory by making noises. Bright colors, like orange or yellow, show that the animal is poisonous.

There are different things that we use that come from the rain forests. Did you know that something you are using right now might have come for the rain forest.? For example some foods you eat come from the rain forest. They are fruits, nuts, spices, coffee, sugar cane, bananas, saps gums, and juices.

Figure 6.7
Alanna's Report on the Rain Forest

Figure 6.7 is a sample of Alanna's writing on "The Rain Forest" that Betty uses to invite conversation using some of the questions above. For example, Betty might ask students to consider Alanna's lead, choice of words, and style of writing.

Betty also shares Knud's Table of Contents page and Chapter One to help students appreciate a different approach to report writing. For ex-

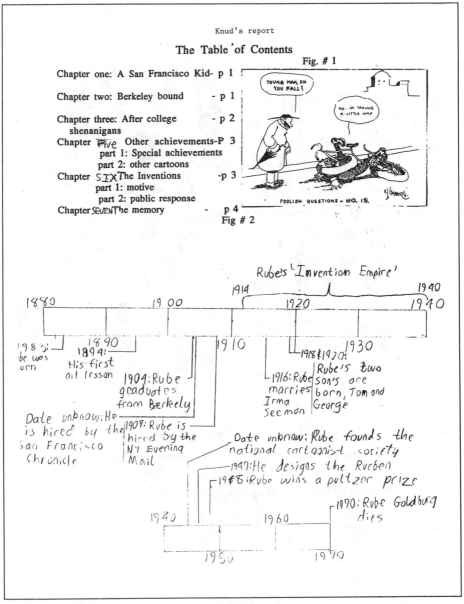

Figure 6.8
Knud's report

ample, Knud definitely shows his own unique researcher's voice incorporating a time-line and cartoons in his writing about inventor Rube Goldburg. See Figure 6.8 & 6.9 below.

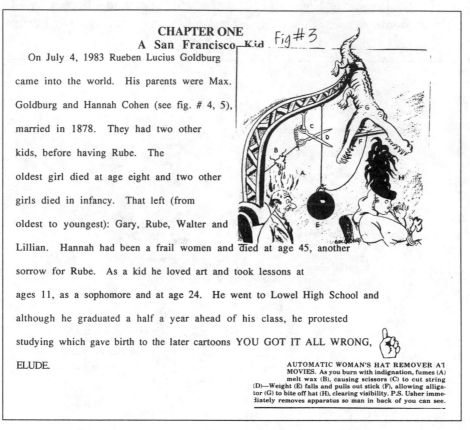

Figure 6.9

Betty uses children's literature to teach reading and writing strategies. She does this by developing five-minute mini-lessons. The following is a sampling of some of her favorite books from which she develops her mini-lessons.

Sample Books	**Focus for Mini-Lesson**
George, Jean Craighead (1972). *Julie of the Wolves*. New York: Harper & Row.	Leads
Taylor, Mildred D. (1976). *Roll of Thunder Hear My Cry*. New York: Dial.	Dialect
London, Jack (1980). *White Fang*. New Jersey: Waterman.	Point of View
Fritz, Jean (1982). *Homesick—My Own Story*. New York: G.P. Putnam.	Flashback
Carroll, Lewis (1981). *Alice's Adventures in Wonderland* and *Through the Looking Glass*. New York: Bantam.	Word Choice
Grahame, Kenneth (1969). *The Wind in the Willows*. New York: Dell.	Characterization
Hamilton, Virginia (1988). *In the Beginning*. San Diego, CA: Harcourt Brace Jovanovich.	Myths (as an example of genre)

The Resource Gathering Process

Betty invites students to help her create a web of all the possible sources they can imagine for finding information to answer their questions. From their previous experiences, students are quick to point out that finding many books is important. To help them stretch in their thinking, Betty asks them to consider other places to find information beyond books. Below is the web she and the students created.

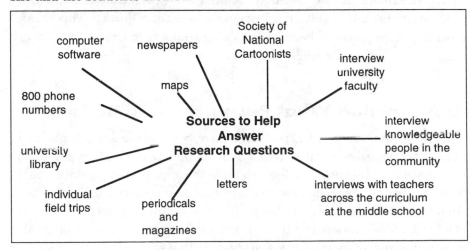

Figure 6.10
The "User-Friendly" Media Specialist

Betty knows that the school library, as well as the public and University of Maine libraries, will be key sources for information. First, she starts on a small scale working collaboratively with her school media specialist. They have formed a partnership in developing a listing of valuable sources and have designed activites that directly relate to the student's research projects. Betty feels that the key to success is her own willingness to work closely with the librarian throughout the research process. Working as a team, rather than simply sending students to the library, has reaped wonderful results! The school library, in fact, becomes the classroom.

Betty holds high expectations for herself, as well as for *all* of her students. She exudes enthusiasm for the library. It's not uncommon to observe Betty involved in her own library research, as well. She later shares all her "finds," not hesitant to admit that some of the sources she found that day were new to her. This modeling and excitement about her own learning is so vital to the success of her approach to research in the classroom; it literally "rubs off" on students! Betty also becomes a helper in supporting her students' search for resources. In her own "travels" around the library she might discover a resource that would be perfect for Susie's paper on the witchcraft trials or Danny's questions about the Civil War. She is very conscious about the ways she helps students, so through the course of their work together she makes sure she touches base in some personal way with each student.

Betty also works closely with the media specialist in helping students to use computer resources and *The Reader's Guide to Periodicals* with ease. For example, they developed a series of question cards about specific information found in *The Reader's Guide to Periodicals* to use as a learning tool. A little competition between two teams plus prizes (a bookmark) encourage all students to become involved in learning to use their library. This careful teaching reaps powerful benefits in freeing students to work in the library with a high degree of confidence and ability.

Determining What Resources Will Be Helpful

Two of the important aspects of research reporting are the ability to gather a wide assortment of books and the ability to decide whether the information in the sources will be useful in the inquiry. Betty asks students how they would approach this task without having to read the entire book from start to finish. Through this line of questioning, she gets a good sense of whether students would pursue this piece of the puzzle by using the table of contents and an index. Betty also observes that students like to take time browsing through a book. Even though they might make use of aides such as the table of contents and index, they do enjoy flipping through an interesting book, looking at photographs, reading the beginning of the book, and simply skimming and scanning for interesting tidbits of information. She encourages students to do this, as they tell her how much other information they can find this way. For instance, the author's style might be particularly fascinating or the language choices or other elements of style might hold a reader's attention, even though the book might not become one of the final resources. Sometimes students remark that they find conflicting information between and among authors.

Students get used to being much more critical about what they read and will search additional sources for confirming information. Betty has learned over time that the skill of being a critical reader has to be discovered by students. She can certainly plant the seeds of this feeling of disequilibrium by choosing several books that offer conflicting information. This leads to a series of questions about the author's credentials, the author's informational sources, copyright date, and audience for the book.

It is also important to guide students through the skimming and scanning process in searching for pertinent information and in note-taking. This is also a time when Betty makes use of student writing and published writing. She prepares overheads of the writing and demonstrates how to quickly skim the material, copying key phrases or bits of information that might answer research questions. For example, using Alanna's or Knud's writing, Betty asks students to read it from the overhead and to generate research questions.

Recording Pertinent Information

As students sift through all of their research materials, they take notes to answer their questions, responding to no more than two questions per page. This strategy makes it easier for students to add to their findings when doing further investigations. It also allows students to cut up their responses and to move the pieces on their desks to help them decide how the written piece will be organized.

On the overhead, Betty takes a sample of one student's cut-up pieces and has students come up and organize the pieces of text in a variety of ways, discussing the pros and cons of each choice. Again, students need to see the process in action, not just to be told how to do it. Over the years, Betty has found that this process of reading and taking notes seems to be easier for students than preparing an abundance of note cards. They enjoy being able to actually manipulate their pieces of data to see what different organizational patterns emerge.

Organizing the Bibliography

Betty is very direct about teaching students how to organize their bibliography of resources. She helps them see connections between their appreciation of a carefully crafted bibliography in a published book and their own. This stage happens early in the research process so that valuable resources are not "lost" along the the way. If a book, journal, or magazine is returned to the library without first recording all pertinent information, that source can become difficult to find later. Students are left scrambling at the last minute for that piece of the research puzzle.

Betty models the bibliographic process by listing books and resources on an overhead and then describes a way to record each one. She includes a sample bibliography for students to keep in their research folders for handy reference.

Organizing Research Questions and Writing an Interesting Lead

Organizing research questions begins as students are ready for that step. Betty teaches a mini-lesson on writing strong and interesting leads using lots of samples of student work on overheads. She finds that with many students this step of writing introductory paragraphs needs reteaching on an individual basis.

At this point, students number their material in the order in which they think it will appear in the final draft. They write a rough copy of their introductory paragraphs or leads to share with their editing/research partner. Betty conferences with each student after this step is completed. In addition, she also finds that students need help with writing concluding paragraphs. Their research and writing styles are all different; it is this uniqueness that makes their reports appreciated and applauded at the final presentation.

Share Circles

When students complete their first draft, they use strategies from the writing workshop and apply them to report writing. They conference with members of their research team or editing partner. At least once a week, students also form a share circle to discuss their writing. Five or six students who wish to share a draft of their report sit in a circle on the floor. All other students sit in a circle around those sharing their pieces. The function of this circle is to listen and learn. Only those who are sharing offer recommendations and ask questions. Betty usually sits away from both circles, listens, and takes notes on the sharing. It is quite obvious that this sharing time is run totally by kids!

Betty asks for a volunteer to lead the circle. She has taught her students a procedure for running share circles that reflects respect for each other. The dialogue goes like this. Deanna volunteers to lead the share circle. Betty says, "I turn the share circle over to you, Deanna." Deanna responds, "Thank you" and proceeds to ask who would like to share first. Phil reads the draft of his report first. Then, Deanna asks for comments and questions. Deanna calls on students, and the process continues with the next student sharing. Students receive feedback on the clarity and organization of their reports, as well as on other aspects about which the writer might ask. They then return to redraft their pieces taking advantage of their classmates' feedback. When asked their opinion of the share circle technique, students are in unanimous agreement that they love this format for sharing, because it is kid-controlled. They are in charge, and that makes all the difference.

Next, Betty conferences with each student, not to hear their pieces read aloud, but to simply listen to what each student has to say about their research questions and findings and to offer suggestions related to content.

After that, students have an editing conference with their editing partner, correcting all mechanical errors they can find. When this step is completed, each student schedules a final editing conference with Betty. She discusses any additional mechanical issues. Students are held responsible for their own checklist of skills they have created. If students have not checked their lists prior to conferencing with Betty, back they go to attend to business!

Decisions about Final Products

As a major component of the research process, students need to identify a variety of ways to share what they have learned. The purpose is to enhance the way they present their findings to the class. Again, Betty uses webbing as a strategy to brainstorm ideas. Below is a sample "generic" product web.

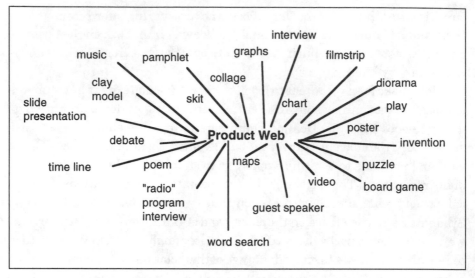

Figure 6.11
"Generic" Product Web

Celebrations

Betty remarks that this final stage of the research process is the most fun for her and the students. This is a time to celebrate all of their hard work as researchers. It is also a time to value, assess, and appreciate the ways in which each student brought his or her individual strengths and gifts to the process. Sharing also gives students an opportunity to learn and grow from each other; it is a time to reflect on some of the unique ways each student viewed the research process and carried it out.

Students prepare to present their findings to the class by writing notes on index cards to be used as cue cards. Betty asks students to brainstorm a list of the kinds of information they think the class would enjoy hearing presented. Students feel a sense of ownership since they generate the list of suggestions to guide the presentations. They came up with the following list of suggestions:

- Title of their research and why they were interested in pursing this research
- Major research questions
- Summary of interesting and fascinating findings
- Sample of the resources they used to answer their questions
- Sharing of product

When students have finished completing their cue cards, they rehearse their presentation with members of the research team. Betty asks students to sign up as to when they would like to present—again, this is another instance of student choice and decision-making. Betty asks the presenter to choose two students to evaluate the presentation using the form in Figure 6.12 below.

PROJECT EVALUATION

NAME _____

PROJECT NAME _____

EVALUATOR _____
☐ Teacher
☐ Friend
☐ Researcher

Read each question and circle the number that best describes your opinions about this project.

	A LITTLE		A LOT
1. Does the researcher really understand the topic ?	1 2	3	4
2. Did the researcher use a variety of resources ?	1 2	3	4
3. Did it hold my attention?	1 2	3	4
4. Is it imaginative and creative?	1 2	3	4
5. Does it show high quality work?	1 2	3	4
6. Is it well organized and easy to follow ?	1 2	3	4
7. Did it answer the major research question ?	1 2	3	4

Figure 6.12

Betty evaluates students' research projects much the same way she evaluates student writing. She and her students assess each project, then discuss their findings and come to a meeting of the minds. The evaluation sheet is attached to a photocopy of the student's research report and sent home for the parents to read and enjoy.

Name _____ Date_____

*RESEARCH REPORT EVALUATION

1=D
2=C-
3=C
4=B-
5=B
6=A-
7=A

_____ INFORMATION-OVERALL CONTENT COVERED.

_____ PRESENTATION-ORGANIZATION OF REPORT.

_____ ORAL REPORT-ORAL PRESENTATION.

_____ JOURNAL-WEBS, QUESTIONS, ROUGH DRAFT

_____ BIBLIOGRAPHY-REPORTING RESOURCES USED.

_____ HANDWRITING-OVERALL HANDWRITING-
                           INCLUDING JOURNALS, DRAFTS, FINAL REPORTS.

_____ MECHANICS-SPELLING, PARAGRAPHING, USE OF
                           QUOTES, ETC.

Comments: _____

_____

_____

Parent comments: _____

_____

_____

Parent's signature _____

*Teacher may choose to give individual scores or arrive at a composite score.

Figure 6.13

Students share their findings and products that enhance their final presentation. Here we see an array of product choices—a video, slide presentation, and even a guest speaker! Betty also videotapes each presentation for viewing and critiquing later with students. She finds that students need feedback in a variety of ways in order to improve on each component of the research process. Betty's gentle and caring way is reflected in the trust students place in both her and the process. Students never feel threatened or made to feel humiliated or ashamed of their work; whether it be alone in discussing the report and videotape or in front of the class. Student researchers write as experts in terms of their inquiry topic (Weis & Stewart-Dore, 1986). Students work hard and aspire to great things in this class because Betty establishes a climate of mutual respect, caring, and cooperation.

This kind of sharing and celebrating gives students both an audience for their work and an opportunity to talk about what they have learned from each other in terms of pursuing their next research project. For instance, Lindy comments that she would like to conduct interviews for her next project on the environment. She's not clear on what aspect of the environment she wants to study, but she learned so much from Randy's report on the Penobscot River and his interviews with people who live along the river, such as the Penobscot Indians, that she would like to do something in a similar vein. She learned how important it is to investigate local environmental issues.

Finally, the research process offers students an opportunity to develop habits of mind. Here is a sampling of questions Betty has found successful in tapping their metacognitive activity or their ability to articulate what they are learning.

Habits of Mind that Students Learn as Researchers

- Ways to identify topics of interest
- Strategies for formulating questions about a topic
- Learning about a broad range of informational sources
- How to skim and scan for pertinent information
- Reasons for being critical readers and consumers of information
- Ways to use webbing to brainstorm ideas
- Using writing process strategies for report writing
- How to think through the writing and format of a research report
- Ways to take notes and organize information
- How to work collaboratively and cooperatively with each other

- Ways to value and appreciate the strengths of each member of the learning community

- Determining a multitude of ways to enhance the written report with a product

- Strategies for sharing, giving, and receiving feedback in positive ways

- Refining presentation skills

- Developing and sustaining a spirit of inquiry and joy of learning

Tchudi (1991) offers "Some principles of interdisciplinary learning" that reflect important principles of teaching and learning in Betty's classroom:

- Learning must be linked to students' concerns, values, and questions; it cannot be simply centered around the structures of disciplines.

- Disciplinary and interdisciplinary knowledge is not random or unstructured; at best, it meshes with young people's interests by helping them understand the world.

- Learning through questioning, firsthand experience, and experimentation creates more complete mastery then does passive reception of information through texts, lectures, or even audio-visual presentations.

- Linking learning across disciplines and subject areas leads to greater learning than teaching the disciplines in isolation.

- Interdisciplinary learning can be pursued in subject-centered classes (for example, math, science, history) at virtually any time.

- Interdisciplinary inquiry is open-ended and intellectually engaging for learners of all ages (p. 20).

Coming Full Circle

Students are now in a position to begin the research cycle again. Many students complete as many as five or six reports throughout a year. This is an on-going process; one in which students learn a plethora of strategies for pursuing their own questions, as well as providing a sort of kaleidoscopic view of themselves as learners and researchers as they investigate each new topic.

As students discover answers to their questions, Betty often hears, "Mrs. Robinson, Guess what I found out!! Did you know that?" Betty sums up the experience by saying, "We discover these wonderful new things together as a learning community. Much of what I learn from students is new information for me, and I tell students that! In fact, I can honestly say that I learn something new everyday from my students. This classroom is an exciting place for me to be!"

REFERENCES

Christie F. (1986). Learning to mean in writing. In Nea Stewart-Dore (Ed.). *Writing and reading to learn*. Rozelle, Australia: Primary English Teaching Association.

Galton, M., & Williamson, J. (1992). *Group work in the primary classroom*. New York: Routledge, Chapman and Hall.

Graves, D. (1989). *Investigating nonfiction*. Portsmouth, NH: Heinemann.

Johnson, D. W., & Johnson, R.T. (1994). *Learning together and alone: Cooperative, competitive, and individualistic learning* (4th Ed.). Englewood Cliffs, NJ: Prentice-Hall.

Martinello, M. L., & Cook, G. E. (1994). *Interdisciplinary inquiry in teaching and learning*. New York: Macmillan.

Ogle, D. (1986). K-W-L: A teaching model that develops active reading of expository text. *The Reading Teacher, 39*, 564–570.

Tchudi, S. (1991). *Travels across the curriculum: Models for interdisciplinary learning*. New York: Scholastic.

Watson, D., Burke, C., & Harste, J. (1989). *Whole language: Inquiring voices*. New York: Scholastic.

Weis, J. with Stewart-Dore (1989). Writing and reading to learn together. In Nea Stewart-Dore (Ed.). *Writing and reading*. Rozelle, Australia: Primary English Teaching Association.

CHILDREN'S BOOKS

Carroll, L. (1981). *Alice's adventures in wonderland and through the looking glass*. New York: Bantam.

Fritz, J. (1982). *Homesick—my own story*. New York: G.P. Putnam.

George, J. C. (1972). *Julie of the wolves*. New York: Harper & Row.

Grahame, K. (1969). *The wind in the willows*. New York: Dell.

Hamilton, V. (1988). *In the beginning*. San Diego, CA: Harcourt Brace Jovanovich.

London, J. (1980). *White fang*. New Jersey: Waterman.

Taylor, M. D. (1976). *Roll of thunder hear my cry*. New York: Dial.

CHAPTER 7

Student and Teacher Co-Created Integrated Curriculum

P. Elizabeth Pate, Elaine Homestead, and Karen McGinnis

Curriculum integration and learning by solving real problems go hand-in-hand. This can be accomplished by middle level students and teachers co-creating problem-centered, hands-on learning projects that focus on issues relevant to students. Recently, three educators decided to set up a school year around the notion of student and teacher co-created integrated curriculum. These educators, two eighth grade middle school teachers and an associate professor of middle level education, made significant changes to connect the curriculum to the students.

The process of change began by discussing curriculum issues, two-member teams, flexible scheduling, teaching and learning strategies, and student and teacher motivation. We reflected upon the ideas of Beane (1990), Dewey (1990), Jacobs (1989), Wigginton (1985), and those suggested by the Carnegie Council on Adolescent Development (1989). We discussed, debated, and philosophized issues related to schooling.

As a result, Elaine and Karen became teachers on a two-member team in a middle school rather than their former five-member team. Developing a democratic classroom, one in which students are actively involved in decision making, with their 60 students was a top priority. Implementing integrated curriculum, one that connects all aspects of the curriculum (the working world, subject content and skills, and social skills) for students and teachers, was not left to chance but actively pursued (Pate, McGinnis, & Homestead, in press).

We developed a survey for the upcoming eighth graders to find out more about their interests and wants. We asked them to tell us how they learned best, what concerned them most at school, what they would like to learn, what they would change about school if they could. We used their responses to help in our initial conceptualization of integrated curriculum. The upcoming eighth graders responded that they wanted less "book work" and more "projects." They indicated they wanted to study more about issues that were important to them. They wanted to know about the current issues and less about the past.

Since Elaine and Karen were in the throes of curriculum restructuring in their county, they chose to organize the themes around social studies and science. Language arts was incorporated by having students focus on the skills of writing, reading, speaking, researching, as well as poetry and novel studies. Dramatic and fine arts activities such as plays, puppetry performances, and art presentations were chosen by the students in their performance assessments. Mathematics was taught both as a separate skills class and by incorporating various mathematics concepts into integrated themes. Units were based on student interest and on state-mandated curriculum.

Our integrated curriculum included four units of study: Human Migration, Human Interactions and the Environment, Human/Civil Rights and Responsibilities, and Communities of the Future. Each of the units began with a focus on the individual students' connection to a topic, shifting to a local, state, national, and world historical perspective, and culminating with considerations of current and future implications for all levels of society.

At the beginning of the year, we modeled theme development. We wanted to show students the process of developing curriculum. As the year progressed, we collaborated more and more on developing themes with our students. The final theme of the year, Communities of the Future, was mostly student-developed.

It was important to have a democratic classroom in which students were to have input and were given choices. Introducing democracy in our classroom included student and teacher collaboration on the team management plan, grading policy, parent communication, and curriculum. It meant providing opportunities for student choice. It did not mean letting students dictate everything that went on.

In this chapter, we discuss several of the thematic units that were co-created by eighth grade students and ourselves. It is important to recognize that integrated curriculum looks different in every classroom and across years. It is our hope that the reader can increase his or her understanding of student and teacher co-created integrated curriculum by having a glimpse at some of our units.

Sample Themes

HUMAN MIGRATION

For the first thematic unit of the school year, we chose the topic of human migration. We chose this topic for two reasons. First, so our students could gain a perspective of why they are where they are, and second, to further understand diversity. The overarching questions for the unit were "How has my world been affected by human migration?" and "What will be the implications of human migration on me in the future?"

We began by asking each student why he or she was living in our particular community. Their answers included such things as employment opportunities, family ties, and the search for political and religious freedom. The students discovered that even though they were culturally, ethnically, and economically diverse, their families all had similar reasons for moving to our community.

This realization led to the need for them to find out who their ancestors were, where their ancestors came from, why they left, when and where they arrived in the United States, and where they are now. In order to find out this information, the students researched their family history with the goal of writing and illustrating their family's story of migration to America. In the stories, they included the interrelationship between the environment and human migration. For example, students researched wind patterns, ocean currents, climate, weather, topography, and natural resources and their effect on human migration.

The students had a choice on how they wanted to present their family stories to the class. Several students created Nickelodeons, boxes with rolling picture frames. Some Nickelodeons began with maps of their family's country of origin, followed by pictures and descriptions of their native traditions and customs, the event which led to their migration, their trip over to America, where they embarked, and a picture of their new home. Other students chose to write and illustrate stories of their family's migration to America.

Once the students were personally connected to the topic of human migration throughout their personal histories, it was easier to answer the next question: "How are world human migration patterns correlated with the settlement and growth of Georgia and the United States?" The next task for the students was to study the historical reasons why our country and state were colonized. Topics of study included early exploration and colonization and how the science concepts of wind patterns and ocean currents determined the location of settlement in the Americas as well as how topography, climate, and natural resources influenced westward movement within our state and country.

As the students realized that human migration into our country has continued throughout our country's history, they began to wonder how human migration might affect their future. They posed questions such as,

"Why are people continuing to migrate to the United States?"

"Where are people migrating from?"

"How will continued migration affect my employment opportunities, my standard of living, and where I might live?"

"What impact will future migration have on our environment?"

From these student-generated questions, research projects were developed. Groups of students chose migration "hot spots"; studied the reasons for migration to the United States and Georgia, in particular; brainstormed possible implications for the future; and shared their findings with the class.

HUMAN INTERACTIONS AND THE ENVIRONMENT

One of the integrated units stemmed from student concerns about the condition of our environment. As a large group, we discussed issues such as ozone pollution, erosion due to clear cutting ("selective harvesting"), acid rain, and the quality of air and water. We then discussed these issues in relationship to the Georgia environment and brainstormed a list of concerns. From this list we developed the unit "Human Interactions and the Environment."

It was important for the students to find out who (locally and nationally) was responsible for regulating and monitoring Georgia's environment and how they, as teenage citizens, could make a difference. Each group was responsible for educating other team members via a multi-media presentation about their chosen concerns. The students soon realized that they needed extensive earth science and social studies content background to better understand their concerns, teach others, and devise plans to help make a difference regarding their selected environmental problems.For examples, they needed to know about: The chemical structure of ozone, erosion and deposition, underground water systems, local and state agencies and their duties and responsibilities, demographics, and physical/cultural map skills.

Because the textbooks did not have the information the students needed, they were forced to seek current outside-of-class resources. They scoured the media center for information, invited guest speakers, contacted state agencies for up-to-date information, wrote a proposal to the principal to fund an on-line computer information service, and planned fact-finding missions off school campus.

For example, a group of five girls were especially concerned about "Animal Testing." The girls wanted to find answers to the following questions:

1. What is animal testing?

2. Why do laboratories use animal testing?

3. What are some of the animals used in animal testing?

4. What type of research is conducted and what kinds of tests are run on animals?

5. Why do laboratories believe it is necessary to use animals in animal research and testing?

6. Why are some people against using animals in laboratory research?

7. What are some of the damaging effects towards the animals?

8. What is animal research?

9. Approximately how much money is spent yearly on animal testing and research?

10. How does animal testing and research affect the world around us?

11. What types of products are tested on animals?

The groups of students read journal and newspaper articles, books, and pamphlets on animal testing in order to obtain background knowledge. Daily entries were logged in journals and kept for a portfolio. Sample journal entries included such things as: "Today we made a calendar to keep track of when our assignments are due." and "Today we worked on writing petitions and making phone calls." Letters were written to various companies involved in animal testing. Problems in animal testing were discussed and alternatives were supplied. Posters and opinion sheets were prepared for class and school distribution. A presentation (using a "backboard") was made to other eighth graders in the school. The group of girls developed a rubric (a form of a checklist) to evaluate what they felt was important content in their topic.

Other projects that students shared for the unit included a narrated slide-presentation; student-made videos; a puppet show; photo displays (One group catalogued their efforts to mobilize their neighborhood to clean up a nearby lake); models, charts and graphs of statistical data; and student-generated computer programs detailing pertinent environmental information.

HUMAN/CIVIL RIGHTS AND RESPONSIBILITIES

The democratic process became evident in the unit Human/Civil Rights and Responsibilities. In this integrated unit, we examined the relationships between past, present, and future human and civil rights issues from the 1600s to the present. We asked students to develop a timeline as an assessment to demonstrate their understanding. The classroom became totally silent. Students looked at each other and then at us. They said they had learned too much for a "simple" timeline. So we asked them how they wanted to demonstrate what they had learned. The students brainstormed and the ideas started flowing. They all wanted to do something "big." The students ended up constructing a "Living History Timeline" based on historical events of human and civil rights. They chose issues and events to re-enact. They wrote scripts and created scenery backdrops. The "Living History Timeline" depicted eleven events ranging from the Salem Witch Trials to Bosnia/Herzegovina.

COMMUNITIES OF THE FUTURE

The final unit of the year was Communities of the Future. This unit incorporated governmental/economic systems and astronomy. It required the students to include content thoughtfully and to apply skills learned from the other units we studied over the year.

The students worked on research skills (e.g. developing good research questions, using a variety of resources, interpreting information from a variety of media, writing to communicate information—including using the Mac Lab for word processing and creating HyperCard stacks and SlideShows. They utilized social skills (e.g. group processing, cooperation, teamwork, listening, contributing ideas, encouraging others). And they incorporated organizational skills (e.g. organizing work, keeping neat records, developing plans, revising plans, and using time wisely) into their curriculum planning.

We wanted the students to practice working on skills that would help them be self-directed and contributing members of a cooperative team. The students had to develop and implement a daily plan of action. Because we had a large block of time (3 hours) in which to work (and if not careful, in which to goof off) and because 14 year-olds have not had much experience budgeting their time and planning ahead, we developed with the students a daily planning guide. We also coopertively developed a checklist that students used daily to evaluate their work regimen.

We wanted our students to practice reflective thinking. Student became more aware of what they were doing that was contributing to their groups' success or causing the group to be unsuccessful. The reflective thinking became writings that were kept in personal journals.

The topic of developing a community of the future was a natural for generating a product of some kind. We realized that it is natural for youngsters to want to spend their time on the fun part of a project (the product) and ignore the most important part (the process). It was clear to all of us from the beginning that student evaluations (and thus their grades) would be generated from the process, as well as the product generated from that learning.

Each community of the future had to include a governmental and economic system. Reasons for choices had to be given. Background information was needed on various types of governmental and economic systems. Choosing the right form of governmental/economic system for their community of the future was an important component of the unit for students. Because the governmental and economic systems of a society reflect the attitudes and values of its people, it was important that each group member have a personal opinion about the governmental and economic system chosen for their community.

Systems studies included monarchy, oligarchy, democracy, dictatorship, capitalism, and socialism. Students read information packets about each system, discussed them as a class, and clarified any misconceptions or ambiguities. To check for understanding, each student completed a Comparative Governments Data Retrieval Chart. They listed each form of government and wrote the advantages and disadvantages of each. They compared and contrasted their responses with other student responses.

Students also gained a working knowledge of capitalism and socialism. We developed a list of advantages and disadvantages for each economic system and discussed them at length. Each student was asked to choose which form of governmental/economic system s(he) thought was best and tell why based on his or her own attitudes and values. With this background knowledge, students were ready to contribute their ideas for the next task.

The students were then asked the question, "What is needed for society to function?" We listed ideas, grouped ideas, labeled them, and created concept maps of ideas. The next question asked was, "If you were going to begin a new colony/community in the future, where would you go?" Two "givens" were provided:

1. The colony/community must be completely isolated.

2. You will never return home.

The class came up with these possible locations for communities of the future:

> another planet
>
> an island
>
> underground
>
> under water/ocean
>
> the biosphere
>
> the moon

We had each student get out a piece of paper and list his or her first, second, and third choices of where the community would be located. Groups were formed according to student choices as well as the needs/strengths of the group members. After the groups were formed, we brainstormed a list of beginning questions. The questions were listed and rearranged in the order in which they could be answered logically. Organizational skills and goal setting were discussed frequently during group processing.

The "communities of the future" groups then developed duties and responsibilities for themselves. They pretended they were the leadership team for the expedition. They decided who had what roles and they developed a duties and responsibilities list for each role. As each task was finished, a briefing of the task went into a group portfolio.

Many science and social studies concepts and skills were integrated into the "Communities of the Future" unit, as well as the use of computer technology. Some of the concepts and skills included: biomes, topographical maps, latitude and longitude, climate, density/mass/gravity, planetary orbits/revolution/rotation, light years, metric to English conversions, knots to mph, governmental/economic systems, energy sources, crop yields/hydroponic farming/pollination, transportation, site planning, computer simulations and graphics, and so on.

Most of the groups decided their final product for this unit was a model of their community and a scale drawing. The group presentations for the Communities of the Future were wonderful. The communities were well thought out, and the scale drawings and models were, for the most part, quality work. Each group's community had a government and economic system, a vision for education, shelter, energy sources(s), food sources(s), division of labor, and much more. Since the students learned best when actively involved, this unit was a great way to end the school year.

Conclusion

The process of student and teacher co-created integrated curriculum was a learning experience for us all. We learned that getting started on units was difficult for some of the students. Some students wanted to get right to work and not spend much time on planning and preparation. They had a difficult time understanding that more time spent on planning and preparation translated into less time fixing problems. We learned that developing a trusting relationship and a democratic classroom takes time and work and give and take. We learned that the process went more quickly and smoothly when we gave our students something tangible to edit, critique, or vote on rather than asking them to create something from scratch. And we learned that when middle school students and teachers co-created problem-centered, hands-on learning projects that focus on issues relevant to students, curriculum connections can be made successfully.

REFERENCES

Beane, J. A. (1990). *The middle school curriculum: From rhetoric to reality.* Columbus, OH: National Middle School Association.

Carnegie Council on Adolescent Development. (1989). *Turning points: Preparing American youth for the 21st century.* Washington, D.C.: Carnegie Corporation.

Dewey, J. (1990). *The school and society and the child and the curriculum.* Chicago: The University of Chicago Press.

Jacobs, H. H. (Ed.). (1989). *Interdisciplinary curriculum.* Alexandria, VA: Association for Supervision and Curriculum Development.

Pate, P. E., McGinnis, K., & Homestead, E. (in press). Components of coherent curriculum. In J. Beane (Ed.), *Toward a coherent curriculum.* Alexandria, VA: Association for Supervision and Curriculum Development.

Wigginton, E. (1985). *Sometimes a shining moment.* New York: Agathon.

Integrative Learning at the Middle Level: The Building Blocks

PART III — Introduction

I believe   that there is, therefore, no succession of studies in the ideal school curriculum. If education is life, all life has, from the outset, a scientific aspect, an aspect of art and culture, and an aspect of communication. It cannot therefore, be true that proper studies for one grade are mere reading and writing, and that at a later grade, reading, or literature, or science, may be introduced. The progress is not in the succession of studies but in the development of new attitudes towards, and new interests in, experience.

-from *Dewey on Education* selections with an Introduction and Notes by Martin S. Dworkin. New York, NY: Teachers College, Columbia University, 1959, p. 27.

The last section of this book is about the building blocks for curriculum integration. It provides resources and suggests ways of using them in an integrated curriculum and presents a way to think about the learning and inquiring. In Chapter 8, Yvonne Siu-Runyan, professor of literacy education who is currently working with middle school teachers on integrated curricula, discusses the benefits of using literature. She suggests that all genres ought to be used—even picture books. Each genre—realistic fiction, nonfiction, fantasy, historical fiction, poetry, picture books, multicultural/multiethnic literature, traditional literature (folktales, myths, etc.)—provide information in different ways and show students various perspectives and ways of thinking. Siu-Runyan also provides excellent resources teachers can use as they plan their integrated curriculum projects.

Helping students develop "big understandings" is the focus of Chapter 9. Based upon their experiences with developing integrated curricula for a National Science Foundation grant, Debbie Powell and Dick Needham offer a way to think about the concepts or generalizations important for integrated curriculum projects. Through their work with teachers, they discovered that when teachers do not consider the "big understanding(s)" of an integrated curriculum project, they have difficulties planning meaningful instructional activities for their students. They also remind us that when developing integrated curriculum, teachers must not forget to consider and involve the students. In addition, they suggest that an integrated curriculum *demands* a different kind of evaluation process—one that asks students to "...demonstrate their understandings not only through the connections they make in their actual projects, but also by what they say and write."

In Chapter 10, Service Learning is discussed. Elaine Andrus, coordinator of service learning for the state of Colorado, aptly describes service learning and its potential for involving middle school students in curriculum that meets their personal concerns and social issues. Also, Andrus draws many parallels between service learning and educational reforms such as Turning Points, Standards-Based Education, Goals 2000. Included in this chapter are excellent resources for educators interested in intetgrating service learning into the middle school curriculum.

And finally, in Chapter 11, Barbara Whinery and John Swaim, former educators at the middle level, and professors of middle level education, present an annotated list of selected resources teachers will find helpful as they learn, plan, and implement middle school integrated curricula. Take special note of the resources on evaluation and teacher as researcher, for these two topics are important when developing integrated curricula.

CHAPTER 8

Using Literature to Inquire and Learn

Yvonne Siu-Runyan

"I didn't know that Lincoln was a Republican and that he had several children and one died."

-a female sixth grade student

"I had no idea that the Koreans were involved in World War II."

-a male seventh grade student

"I didn't realize that a lot of the problems we face today were also faced by our ancestors."

-a female eighth grade student

How did the students come to these understandings? Through reading and discussing literature, not just by reading and learning information from subject area textbooks.

While many experts (Nat Hentoff, 1984; Paul Gagnon, 1989) agree that textbooks fail to tell the full stories, many well-meaning adults ask, "But don't textbooks provide useful information? I learned from textbooks when I was in school. Wouldn't it be easier if everyone just read the same information in the textbooks? Besides, it's more cost-effective, easier to test, and certainly easier to manage when only one textbook is used for each subject area. Besides, shouldn't the language arts teachers, not content area teachers, be responsible for literature? After all, what do content area specialists know about literature?"

In answer to these questions, Tunnell and Ammon (1993) write, "Textbook publishers, sensitive to special interests, have reduced spirited moments in history filled with human joy and pathos to bland accounts of wars and battles, names and dates, places and populations" (p. vii). And so, while students might know the facts related to historical events, they too often do not have the background knowledge or a deep understanding of the impact of the events and how they have affected people's lives then and now. Often, the information in content area textbooks does not provide the contextual information needed to deeply understand historical events and why they are important.

The same concerns that Tunnel and Ammon voice about only using textbooks in content area classes are also shared by Elleman (1992). On the importance of using trade books in the science curriculum, she writes, "...the content should transport children to new horizons, provide diverse view-points on controversial matters, and discuss interrelationships between topics. Children should be taught early on that there are nearly always two sides to any issue or event, and opposing viewpoints should be introduced. They should also learn that rarely do events happen or people exist in vacuums and that connections between the two are essential" (p. 32).

Besides concern that many textbooks provide only cursory information, which does not help students really understand the complexities of the historical events or the scientific information, there is much discussion and movement toward curriculum integration as a way to transform schools from "...fragmented, departmentalized, or isolated instructional periods to inte-grated contexts..." (Lipson, Valencia, Wixson, and Peters, 1993, p. 253). This notion that improved teaching and learning might be accomplished through curriculum integration (Dewey, 1933; Jacobs, 1989; Drake, 1993; Fogarty, 1991), especially at the middle school level (Beane, 1993; Vars, 1991; Stevenson and Carr, 1993) is not novel. In order to involve students in a curriculum that *is* integrated, many diverse resources—in particular, fiction and nonfiction trade books—are needed. Literature provides the context for understanding the significance of facts. In this way, students are able to transform knowledge into personally useful and meaningful tools for ex-panding their understanding of the world and themselves.

The Importance of Literature
in Inquiring and Learning

"The first and best reasons for using literature stem from its aesthetic and personal values" (Hickman and Cullinan, 1989, p. 4). Outstanding literature is an art form and, like all art forms, literature has incredible power to move us—to touch us deeply. Literature informs and entertains, but, more importantly, awakens feelings. When a piece of literature touches our emotions and perceptions, we become more human. As Huck (1982) states, "Reading and discussing . . . books is one way of humanizing our children. I am not so naive as to think literature will save the world, but I do believe it is one of the things that makes this world worth saving" (p. 316).

Countless young adolescents have read Paulsen's *Hatchet*, only to ask for another book like it. In fact, Ben, one of my former students who became a fluent reader in grade five, read *Hatchet* because other students kept talking about it. When Ben finished reading *Hatchet*—the first book he read independently—he offered, "The kids were right, Yvonne. This is a good book. Do you have another book like this one?" That day, I silently thanked Gary Paulsen for writing the book *Hatchet*, for it was this book which helped Ben to become a reader.

Literature also widens our world view. Literature provides students with the opportunity to participate in new experiences, meet new people, go to new places, and see new things. Carefully selected literature can illustrate the contributions and values of the many diverse cultures found in the student's immediate world and beyond. Most students are not able to: visit the far East; participate in an archaeological dig; go on a wild river rafting trip down the rapids of the Colorado River; or have a conversation with Abraham Lincoln about his life. Nevertheless, while first-hand experiences are preferable but not always possible, students can learn about places like Japan, find out what goes on during an archaeological dig, experience the perils of river rafting, and find out about Abraham Lincoln through good books. Literature can be the next best thing to first-hand experiences. Literature gives readers a way to cross the bridges of centuries and cultures. It supports all areas of inquiry and learning.

A discussion about the values of literature must also include the role literature plays in nurturing, developing, and expanding the imagination. Books can take students into worlds that stimulate the mind and soul and give them materials for dreaming and thinking. This is important in the age of television. Television is very explicit in depicting life and thus students have limited abilities to imagine, visualize, and see with their inner eyes— so important in learning from print.

And finally, a major educational benefit of literature is its influence on student writing. Separate studies by DeFord (1981), Eckhoff (1983), and Mills (1974) found that the stories students wrote reflected characteristics of the materials used for their reading instruction. Those who read basal texts produced simple, repetitious stories. Those who read literature used more complex sentences and interesting storylines. In other words, whether consciously or unconsciously, students are mentored by the authors they read.

A SPECIAL MESSAGE FOR TEACHERS

As you read the following sections of this chapter, please keep in mind that you may be a novice or an expert at curriculum integration or somewhere in between and still be able to use literature to support student inquiry and learning. That is, you do not have to be a teacher who has a completely integrated curriculum. Although this may be the ultimate and final goal, while you are learning how to integrate curriculum, you might want to start small by taking one step at a time. For instance, when studying about World War II, you may want to spend some time reading aloud and discussing books which depict the war from various perspectives. You may also want to bring in a variety of books—picture books, chapter books, informational books, even poetry—students can use as resources to investigate the various aspects of World War II. Examples of excellent books from which middle school students will learn about World War II, the peoples involved, and different perspectives on the war:

1. Japanese American

    Yoshiko Uchida's *The Bracelet* (picture book winner, New York Times)

    Sheila Hamanaka's *The Journey* (picture book)

    Graham Salisbury's *Under the Blood-Red Sun* (chapter book)

2. Child of an American Soldier

    Deborah Kogan Ray's *My Daddy Was a Soldier* (picture book)

3. European Jewish

    Karen Hesse's *Letters from Rifka* (IRA Young Adult Chapter Book Award)

    Shulamith Levey Oppenheim's *The Lily Cupboard* (picture book)

    Lois Lowry's *Number the Star* (Newbery Award Winner)

    Margaret Wild's *Let the Celebrations Begin!* (picture book)

4. Japanese

    Yoko Kawashima Watkin's *So Far from the Bamboo Grove* (chapter book)

    Eleanor Coerr's *Sadako* (picture book)

    Junko Morimoto's *My Hiroshima* (picture book)

    Yukio Tsuchiya's *Faithful Elephants: A True Story of Animals, People and War* (picture book)

5. Allegory of the Holocaust

    Eve Bunting's *Terrible Things* (short chapter book)

Use ALL the Various Types and Genres of Literature

PICTURE BOOKS ARE NOT ONLY FOR YOUNG CHILDREN

A long-held tenet, widely accepted by teachers and students alike, and difficult to dislodge, is that picture books are appropriate only for the young child. Like tricycles, crayons, and blocks, it is assumed that picture books will be replaced by more sophisticated materials like chapter books and encyclopedias as the child grows into a young adolescent. But are picture books only for young children?

An examination of picture books reveals that not all are intended for the young child. Hall (1990) states, "The subtleties of language, art, and at times, the subjects found in a number of picture books are beyond the comprehension and appreciation of the very young child" (p. 3). This perspective has also been voiced by Children's and Adolescent Literature experts Jenks (1992), Bishop and Hickman (1992), and middle school teachers Reif (1992) and Benedict (1992).

So what are the values of using picture books in the middle school integrated curriculum? When answering the question: Why picture books? Bishop and Hickman (1992, pp. 4–7) respond with the following explanation. Picture books:

1. Are a source of personal pleasure and aesthetic satisfaction for all ages
2. Can teach us through the content (words, pictures, and the story itself)
3. Teach with pictures as well as words
4. Can help students become better readers and writers by hearing and reading them and then thinking about and working with them
5. Can build greater student awareness of language
6. Offer opportunities to explore and learn conventions by which illustrations communicate meaning
7. Present opportunities to examine both form and structure and thus improve one's own writing

Keeping in mind these statements that support the use of picture books, consider using them with middle school students in the following ways:

1. To introduce a new concept or idea

2. To note how the author used words (language) and structure (design) to communicate

3. To teach literary devices (Hall, 1990)

4. To build background knowledge for reading more difficult text

5. To learn how to write nonfiction information in an interesting way

6. To learn how to balance words and illustrations on a final copy to share with others

A discussion about picture books would not be complete without mentioning alphabet books. There are many outstanding alphabet books on the market. They are very different from the ones we read as young children. No longer do alphabet books read: "A is for apple. B is for boy. C is for cat, and so on." Alphabet books today are often stories which are connected through the letters of the alphabet. In addition, the illustrations are feasts for the eyes and the language is rhythmic to the ears. So, while middle school students may in fact consider alphabet books too "babyish" for them, point out how the letters of the alphabet provide an organized way to share information, similar to outlining, as well as the kinds of information the book communicates. Then challenge the students to model their own writing after one of the alphabet book formats they investigated. The students will quickly find out that they can share many different kinds of information through alphabet books.

INFORMATIONAL BOOKS

"Where's that book about animals? I was reading about … and boy was it interesting. I'm not finished yet."

"Did you know that … ?"

"Wow, this is amazing information!"

New worlds, new interests, new horizons, and new ways of thinking lie between the pages of informational books. The secrets of making maple syrup, learning how hummingbirds live, and even information about the care and feeding of newborn animals have all been revealed in attractive, engaging, inviting nonfictional books. In fact, because nonfictional books contain interesting information, many students will read and reread these books over and over again. For my students, this was indeed true. But like other kinds of books, unless the quality is high, students will soon lose interest in reading them.

So what are the criteria for evaluating informational books? According to Huck, Hepler, and Hickman (1993, pp. 663–677), a good informational book is:

1. Accurate and authentic: It is written by someone qualified. It is accurate and up-to-date, and includes significant facts. In addition, it avoids stereotypes, uses facts to support generalizations, makes a distinction between fact and fiction, and avoids anthorpomorphism.

2. Has content and pespective: The focus of the book is clear. The information contained is appropriate for the intended audience. The book encourages critical thinking and illustrates the process of inquiry and the excitement of discovery. In addition, it connects and shows the interrelationships among the facts.

3. Style: The language used is precise and specific in detail. It is clear and direct.

4. Organization: There is a clear arrangement of information. Headings should help the reader organize the information in manageable portions. Included are reference aids for helping readers find information.

5. Illustrations and Format: The illustrations and format should clarify and extend the text. Such things as diagrams and drawings can enliven the text and make it clearer. In addition, captions help readers get maximum information from the illustrations and diagrams.

There are many different kinds of informational books: concept books, informational picture books, photographic essays, identification books, life-cycle books, experiment and activity books, documentaries and journals, survey books, specialized books, and craft and how-to books (Huck, Hepler, and Hickman, 1993, pp. 677-688.) Books like these can serve as curriculum resources and help develop critical thinking. Many nonfictional books not only have better language models than textbooks do, but they also provide much more information about subject matter than many textbooks do.

Implementation of an integrated, holistic curriculum requires a variety of resources, and having nonfiction books in the classroom provide a natural starting place. If children are to become lifelong readers, they should be reading outstanding books not only in their reading and languge arts classes, but in all areas of study. The information contained in trade books can contribute to significant understandings about the personal world of students and the larger world. A selection of informational books can provide the depth and richness not possible in textbooks. In addition, trade books provide information not often contained in textbooks because the process of producing and selecting textbooks takes many months or years.

Another important aspect of using nonfiction books is the variety of perspectives they offer on any given topic. "The availability of several informational books on a single topic is important for teachers to consider, because it presents ready-made opportunities to encourage critical reading. When children's information all comes from one source, they are likely to accept the author's selection and interpretation of facts without question" (Huck, Hepler, and Hickman, 1993, p. 688). Using several books provides students with the opportunity to make comparisons and develop their critical thinking.

TRADITIONAL LITERATURE: LEARNING ABOUT CULTURE

There are several types of traditional literature—folktales, fables, myths, and legends. Folktales, fables, myths, and legends tell us something about the culture from which the stories originated. A study of a particular cultural group is not complete without an examination of its traditional literature.

So how can teachers proceed? One can organize the sharing of traditional literature in two ways—by sharing and discussing several versions of the same tale or by investigating folk literature from a single country or culture. Both approaches work well. However, there are different benefits for students, depending on the avenue taken. When students share and discuss different versions of the same tale, they soon discover that, despite outward cultural differences, many people share similar values. For example, over nine hundred versions of the Cinderella story have been found throughout the world; almost every culture has its own Cinderella story. This understanding will help students realize that perhaps people are more alike than different and share many common values.

On the other hand, when investigating the folk literature from a single country or culture, students learn a great deal about a country and its people, but they also increase their knowledge of the multicultural and diverse heritage of America. This knowledge can lead to an understanding of other cultures, as well as the development of positive attitudes toward other cultures.

Two outstanding textbooks which give detailed information about the traditional literature from various cultures and countries are: *Through the Eyes of a Child* by Donna Norton (Chapter 6: "Involving Children in Traditional Literature") and *Children's Literature in the Elementary School* (fifth edition) by Charlotte S. Huck, Susan Hepler, and Janet Hickman

(Chapter 6: "Traditional Literature"). Both resources have excellent bibliographic information and include outstanding suggestions for how the books might be used in the classroom.

Fantasy Makes Visible Many Aspects of Life

The word "fantasy" is derived from the literal translation of a Greek word that means "a making visible." When discussing the importance of fantasy, Woolsey (1989) offers, "These stories provide profound insights into the realities of our existence. They provide glimpses at the complex answers to our deepest questions: Who am I? Where did I come from? What is my purpose in life? How, then, shall I live today? Thus, readers will be a bit different after entering the imaginative vision of the fantasist. As we read fantasy we are extended and stretched toward an understanding of ourselves, our place in the world and the paths that we might take in the future" (p.117).

What does this mean for middle level students? Middle level students are at the perfect age to read fantasy, for they are concerned with questions about what is really right, what is appropriate, and what is basically wrong. Also, middle level students are on a quest to find out who they are and where they fit in society. Because fantasy is *fantastic*, but at the same time, deals with difficult issues, middle level students can easily discuss and explore universal questions and issues. The fantastic situations depicted in fantasy actually help the students step outside of themselves and facilitate the handling of difficult, personal issues. As Stelk (1989) states, "By seeing life in fantasy cast in sharp relief, students can observe from a distance as conflicts are resolved. They can have opinions and thoughts about the conflicts without feeling guilty or thinking the teacher has a hidden motive in getting them to read the book" (p.122).

I have found some outstanding books which I thoroughly enjoyed. These books provided me with new perspectives, and I found their stories lingered in my mind for days after. Here are a few of my favorites:

Lois Lowry's The *Giver* (1994 Newbery Award winner)
Tom Barron's *The Ancient One* (soon to be a movie)
Claude Clement's *The Voice of the Wood*
Madeleine L'Engle's *An Acceptable Time*
Grace Chetwin's *Collidescope*

Because middle level students are at the age where they want and need "meat" or substance in the work they do, bringing them books of fantasy and involving them in meaningful discussions about their themes are important.

Denying middle level students fantasy literature, which helps them to explore who they are and where they fit into society, would be a serious deficit in the middle level curriculum.

HISTORICAL FICTION: LIVING THE PAST THROUGH STORIES

"Through the pages of historical fiction, the past becomes alive" (Norton, 1983, p. 434). This is the primary reason historical fiction should be included in the middle school integrated curriculum. Textbooks are good at providing information about specific events, dates, and even important people and places. Nevertheless, this is not the whole story. Students often wonder why they are studying a certain historical event and will never understand its significance unless the human element is revealed. The importance of historical fiction is that it not only provides the human context for historical events, but, more importantly, it can provide multiple perspectives of the same event, and it invites the reader to enter into an historical discussion that involves making judgments about what happened.

Because middle level students are at a time in their development where issues related to what is "right" and "wrong" are of utmost importance, good historical fiction helps students understand the connections among the past, the present, and the future. As one secondary social studies teacher reports (Benson, 1991), "Like many other history teachers, I have spent too many years turning kids off to history. Using quality literature books in my classes has allowed my students to relive history and provoked in them a life-long interest in the study of history" (p. 21).

REALISTIC FICTION: A WINDOW ON TODAY'S CONTEMPORARY WORLD

Realistic contemporary books are the most criticized and debated among interest groups, parents, and teachers. Because realistic contemporary literature can be about difficult topics, such as growing up, divorce, suicide, death, homosexuality, and so on, teachers need to be aware of the values and mores of the school community. Middle school students will find themselves and the problems with which they deal the subject of many contemporary realistic books. Students need to read books about characters with whom they can relate, who are in situations in which they have found themselves. Reading realistic fiction provides different ways to view and deal with problems. Students learn that they are not alone and that they can live through difficult situations. Here are some topics with selected titles that will interest middle school students:

1. Accomplishments and growing up

   C.S. Adler's *Mismatched Summer*

   Mary Jane Auch's *Out of Step*

   Patti Sherlock's *Four of a Kind*

   Gary Soto's *A Summer Life*

   Kyoko Mori's *Shizuko's Daughter*

2. Family and friends

   A.E. Cannon's *Amazing Gracie*

   Emily Rhoads Johnson's *A House Full of Strangers*

   Ellen Steiber's *Eighth Grade Changes Everything*

   Bruce Brook's *What Hearts?*

   Robert Lehrman's *Separations*

   Mary Downing Hahn's *December Stillness*

   Virginia Euwer Wolff's *Make Lemonade*

When selecting contemporary realistic fiction, teachers must be careful to choose stories that are honest, not sensational. Books which capitalize on the novelty of a subject and sensationalize it should be avoided. If we want students to read realistic fiction that broadens their interests, allows them to experience new adventures, validates them, and shows them ways to cope with difficulties, the books must have integrity.

MULTIETHNIC AND MULTICULTURAL BOOKS: LITERATURE FOR A GLOBAL SOCIETY

Since the founding of America, our country has been made up of diverse ethnic groups. And our nation's diversity has become even more evident in recent years. As we move into the 21st century, we cannot ignore the fact that the world is made up of many different cultural groups, each with a dream of inclusion and a heritage to be celebrated. If we take a look at the current trends in the United States, one can predict that African Americans, Asian Americans, Latinos, and Native Americans will comprise the majority of the school-age population by the next century. Of even greater significance is the anticipated increase in school-aged children of color—from 25 percent to 42 percent by the year 2000 (CMPEAL, 1988).

Also, most people in years past seemed comfortable with the concept of America as a melting pot—a giant cauldron in which immigrants worked at shedding their individual ethnic identities for the larger one of being an

American. Today, however, the situation is different. People are not as willing to ignore their ethnic roots—they want to be recognized as being both an American and someone who has ethnic roots, reflecting individuality and uniqueness. In other words, instead of a melting pot, many people have come to see America as a bowl of flavorful soup or a colorful garden salad, in which the numerous distinctive ingredients each contribute to the combined flavor, more satisfying than any single ingredient could be alone. But what does all this information about diversity and culture mean for us as educators?

In view of these projections and new attitudes, we teachers need to help our students understand and recognize the various peoples who have made significant contributions to the United States and the world. Without an appreciation of those individuals who have helped to shape our world through their significant contributions, the young may well develop an ethnocentric perspective of the world and its many people and cultural groups. The increasing variety of cultural groups in our public schls, along with a renewed interest in and controversy over the content of the literature students read, has revealed the need for a greater variety of ethnic charac-ters and cultural issues in books available to our students. Still, we need to ask ourselves this important question: What kinds of books and how do we determine if they are worthwhile?

Multiethnic and multicultural literature are often confused, even though the differences between the two have been discussed for over 20 years. Multiethnic literature, according to Ruth Kearney Carlson (1972), is the literature about a minority ethnic group with values and characteristics different from the typical white Anglo-Saxon, middle-class persons living in the United States. Multiethnic literature consists of four major categories: Black Americans; Native Americans; Hispanics, including Mexican Ameri-cans, Puerto Ricans, and others of Spanish descent; and Asian Americans, including Chinese Americans, Japanese Americans, Korean Americans, and Vietnamese Americans.

Multicultural literature, on the other hand, has a broader meaning than multiethnic and includes the study of all peoples. For example, a study of multicultural literature would include white ethnic groups, such as Jewish Americans and Italian Americans, along with the study of African Ameri-cans, Latinos, Asian Americans, and Native Americans, as well as the literature of people in other parts of the world.

Why include multiethnic and multicultural literature in the middle school curriculum? Norton (1983) states, "A heightened sensitivity to the needs of all people in American society has led to the realization that the literature program should include literature by, and about, members of all cultural groups. Literature is considered an appropriate vehicle to build respect across cultures, sharpen sensitivity toward individuals, and improve self-esteem" (p. 488). In addition, "Literature can play an important part in helping all … learn about new worlds, new ideas, and different ways of doing things, which will benefit them as human beings" (Rasinski and Padak, 1990).

When selecting multiethnic and multicultural literature, it is important to remember that the selections must be evaluated using the same standards by which other types of literature are evaluated—plot, characterization, setting, author's style, theme, and point of view. In addition, the following guidelines (Ramirez and Ramirez, 1994, pp. 21-22) should be applied:

1. The text should reflect an authentic and sincere portrayal of the way of life of the group portrayed.

2. It should attempt to amend historical errors and omissions by providing accurate information about the group portrayed and individuals who have made contributions to the United States and to the rest of the world.

3. It should replace prejudiced descriptions and stereotyped characters with ones that are more true to life and provide positive images.

4. It should contain illustrations and/or photos that provide a true reflection of the way of life of the group.

5. It should depict women of the group in transition from more traditional to more contemporary roles under the influence of the culture of their new homes in America.

6. It should contain language that provides insight into the culture of the group.

When using multiethnic and multicultural literature with middle school students, Aoki (1981) suggests that adults must lead students in active discussions in the following two ways. First, the discussion should help students understand others by having them take the viewpoint of a character in a story. When students become the character, they embrace the feelings and behaviors of that character and compare them to their own feelings and behaviors in life situations. Second, the discussion should help students search for elements within the story that are related to their own experiences. When students do this, they are better able to identify times when they had similar feelings, needs, and emotions. These two aspects of discussion are important for developing student understanding of cultural differences among groups of people, and, more importantly, of the similarities in universal needs, emotions, and values which *all* cultural groups share.

Some pertinent topics with selected titles which middle level students would enjoy reading and discussing are:

1. Experiencing prejudice

   Laurence Yep's *Dragonwings* and *The Star Fisher* (Chinese American)

   Mildred Pitts Walter's *Mississippi Challenge* (Black American)

   Michael Kronenwetter's *United They Hate: White Supremacist Groups in America* (White Supremacist and the Klu Klux Klan)

   Sara Gogol's *Vatsana's Lucky New Year* (Laotian American)

   Bette Greene's *The Drowning of Stephan Jones* (Homosexuality)

2. Exploring diversity and ethnic relationships

   Lynne Reid Banks' *One More River* (Jewish and Arab)

   David Carkeet's *Quiver River* (Native American—Miwok and White American)

   William Mayne's *Drift* (Native American and White American)

   Emily Cheney Neville's *The China Year* (Chinese and White American)

   Jayne Pettit's *My Name Is San Ho* (Vietnamese refugee and White American teacher)

   Gary Soto's *Pacific Crossing* (Mexican American and Japanese)

   Jacqueline Woodson's *Maison at Blue Hill* (poor Black American girl and rich Black and White American girls)

3. Discovering one's heritage

   Laurence Yep's *Child of the Owl* (Chinese American)

   Evelyn Sibley Lampman's *The Potlatch Family* (Native American)

   Virginia Hamilton's *Zeely* (Black American)

   Sherry Garland's *Song of the Buffalo Boy* (Vietnamese)

   Jean Craighead George's *The Talking Earth* (Native American)

   Johanna Hurwitz's *Class President* (Puerto Rican)

   Graham Salisbury's *Blue Skin of the Sea* (Hawaiian)

As educators we must take every opportunity to use multiethnic and multicultural books so that students have a chance to examine and learn about the cultural experiences, values, and beliefs that are both different from and similar to those of their own culture. Books deemed exceptional in accurately portraying the many cultures of America's peoples will instill in our students the value of diversity so essential to our survival as a multiethnic and multicultural society. To ignore the importance and value of multiethnic and multicultural literature would be irresponsible.

POETRY: THE ESSENCE OF AN OBJECT, A FEELING, OR A THOUGHT

When the word "poetry" is mentioned, many crinkle up their faces and moan, "I hate poetry!" McClure, Harrison, and Reed (1989, p. 174) capture the reasons many of us have for disliking poetry. They write:

> Traditionally, literary response theory has focused on text or author with the influence of reader virtually ignored. As a result, research on response to poetry has been concerned with student ability or inability to discover the "correct" meaning of text. Children are first taught to recognize significant poetic elements, forms, and common poetic devices. It is only after receiving extensive drill on these elements that they are considered ready to study poetry. Children are then shown a course they must follow in order to uncover the "true" meaning inherent in a particular poem. They analyze words and lines as well as search for poetic devices they have been taught to recognize. The teacher acts as arbitrator of what constitutes a correct interpretation, controlling both the procedures followed and the nature of the response. The children are neither expected nor encouraged to bring their personal perspectives to the response process.

"If poetry is disliked by many, why teach it in the first place?" many ask. "After all, there are other more important things teachers can and should spend their time teaching."

While I can understand the argument many have about the value of poetry in the curriculum, involving students with poetry can actually help them become better readers and writers. How? Involvement with poetry increases one's sensitivity and awareness. That is, it helps students become more observant of language and more aware of universal truths. When working with two teachers, Peggy Harrison and Sheryl Reed, researcher Amy McClure (1990) found that students: (1) became better writers—their prose became more poetic, more fluent, and more concise; and (2) became more aware of the nuances of language involved in creating a fine piece of writing.

How did Peggy's and Sheryl's students come to these understandings? No tricks, just responding freely to poetry and writing poetry. Peggy and Sheryl started by sharing lots and lots of outstanding poems with their students. Students were also encouraged to share poems they loved with the rest of the class. Because the students were immersed in poetry and not required to analyze each poem for *the* meaning, they developed an interest in and an appreciation for poems. As their students acquired more experience with poetry, Peggy and Sheryl encouraged them to use their tentative understandings of poetic elements in their own writing. To stimulate their students' thinking and to help them link what they learned about poetry into their own writing, they frequently asked questions like the following:

> *"How could you use what you know about poetry to make your piece more interesting?"*
>
> *"Have you looked closely at that thing you're describing? Have you become a part of it so you really see it?"*

If you are interested in sharing great poetry with your students, I have found the following resources to be excellent:

Myra Cohn Livingston's *Remembering and Other Poems*
Paul B. Janecsko's *Poetspeak*
Paul B. Janeczko's *The Place My Words Are Looking For*
Naomi Shihab Nye's *This Same Sky, A Collection of Poems from Around the World*
Bobbye S. Goldstein's *Inner Chimes, Poems on Poetry*
Dunning, Lueders, and Smith's *Reflections on a Gift of a Watermelon Pickle and Other Modern Verses*

Lee Galda (1993, p. 114) shared this wisdom with us:

Poetry examines emotions and experiences carefully, with honesty and extraordinary clarity of vision, and presents these emotions and experiences through words that sing. Poets work hard to do this, and students, too, can work hard to become poets... something that happens after years of effort. Your classroom can be the place that they take that difficult first step. Hearing, reading, and writing poetry are some of the very best ways to learn about the power and the potential of language. They are also some of the very best ways to learn about one's world and one's self. You don't need gimmicks, elaborate plans, or detailed instructions to involve your students with poetry; you simply need poems and your own obvious pleasure in those poems. If you give your students the gift of a poet's words, they will reap the benefits for the rest of their lives.

Literature Sources

One of the most frustrating things for teachers is not being able to find the "right" resources and books when they need them. This is a very important consideration when using literature in an integrated curriculum. Over the years, I have found some excellent sources of information on available literature. These resources below are by far the best ones I have found for a middle level integrated curriculum.

Adventuring with Books: A Booklist for Pre-K–Grade 6 (tenth edition), edited by Julie M. Jensen and Nancy L. Roser

Beyond Words: Picture Books for Older Readers and Writers, edited by Susan Benedict and Lenore Carlisle

Collected Prespectives: Choosing and Using Books for the Classroom (second edition), edited by Hughes Moir with Melissa Cain and Leslie Prosak-Beres

The Story of Ourselves: Teaching History Through Children's Literature, edited by Michael O. Tunnell and Richard Ammon

Using Nonfiction Trade Books in the Elementary Classroom: From Ants to Zeppellins, edited by Evelyn B. Freeman and Diane Goetz Person

Using Picture Storybooks to Teach Literary Devices: Recommended Books for Children and Young Adults, by Susan Hall

Vital Connections: Children, Science, and Books, edited by Wendy Saul and Sybille A. Jagusch

Your Reading: A Booklist for Junior and Middle School (ninth edition), edited by C. Anne Webb and the Committee on the Junior High Middle School Booklist

Besides these resources, teachers can get information about the newest books available in the following publications:

Booklist and *Journal of Youth Services in Libraries*
c/o American Library Association
50 East Huron Street
Chicago, IL 60611

CBC Features: Lists of Books for Social Studies and Science
c/o The Children's Book Council
67 Irving Place
New York, NY 10003

Language Arts, The ALAN Review, The Journal of Children's Literature
c/o National Council of Teachers of English
1111 Kenyon Road
Urbana, IL 61801

School Library Journal
P.O. Box 1978
Marion, OH 43305-1978

The Colorado Communicator
c/o The Colorado Council of the International Reading Association
P.O. Box 101047
Denver, CO 80250

The Horn Book Magazine
Park Square Building
31 St. James Avenue
Boston, MA 02116

The New Advocate
Christopher-Gordon Publishers
480 Washington Street
Norwood, MA 02062-0000

The Journal of Reading, The Reading Teacher, The Dragon Lode
c/o International Reading Assocation
800 Barksdale Road, P.O. Box 8139
Newark, DE 19714-8139

The WEB
Martha L. King Center for Language and Literacy
Department of Educational Theory and Practice
29 West Woodruff Avenue
Columbus, OH 43210-1177

And finally, middle school teachers will be especially interested in the following resources, for they are books written with middle level teachers in mind. These resources have a plethora of books listed along with information about how they can be used with students across the curriculum in meaningful and purposeful ways.

Coming to Know: Writing to Learn in the Intermediate Grades, by Nancie Atwell

In the Middle: Writing, Reading, and Learning with Adolescents, by Nancie Atwell

Lasting Impressions: Weaving Literature into the Writing Workshop, by Shelley Harwayne

Seeking Diversity: Language Arts with Adolescents, by Linda Rief

Teaching Multicultural Literature in Grades K-8, edited by Violet J. Harris

Using Literature in the Middle Grades: A Thematic Approach, by Joy F. Moss

The resources listed are only a sampling of the many superb ones that are available. As you look for books to use in an integrated curriculum, don't forget to consult one of your most useful resources—your school media specialist. Engage him or her in your search for books. You might even inform the media specialist about the topics you and your students are planning to study so that he or she can put a class collection together for you. Another useful activity might be to involve students in putting together resources for future use. As students study about a particular topic or concept, have them develop a bibliographical resource which can then be shared with other teachers and students. This will involve them in purposeful and meaningful reading and writing for a real audience. Another way to engage students with literature is to have the students record books they especially like onto audio tape for other students and parents to enjoy.

End Notes

"Most of what children learn in school is concerned with *knowing;* literature is concerned with *feeling*. We cannot afford to educate the head without the heart" (Huck, 1989, p. 254). If we are to help students become wise, not just knowledgeable, then we must address the need for literature across the curriculum. While books provide information, they more importantly create feelings and in the process educate and transform the mind and heart.

Teachers who want to include literature in their curriculum can start without knowing everything about using literature. The following recommendations are easy to follow, do not take a lot of preparation or knowledge, and can do much to transform your classroom.

First, read to your students every day. Share all kinds of literature—picture books, chapter books, fiction books, and nonfiction books. Hearing excellent literature can develop in your students an appreciation for the language of literature and the conventions of stories.

Second, bring a wide variety of books into the classroom which deal with the topic or concept being studied. Do book talks about them, and encourage students to self-select and read the book(s) which interest them. Encourage them to connect the information learned in the content area textbooks with the literature they read.

Third, provide time for students to talk with one another about the books they read. Instead of having students write book reports to be shared only with the teacher, brainstorm with students about novel and interesting ways they can share the books with others. After all, there is no better advertisement for a good book than another student's enthusiasm.

Fourth, search out books. Read them and notice how much you benefited from reading the book. Then share your perceptions and what you learned from the book with your students.

Fifth, don't forget to start small. Pick one thing to do. Take little steps as you move towards curriculum integration. Then as you feel comfortable, expand.

And sixth, ask questions and don't be afraid to talk with other teachers. Many are in the same situation as you. Form a support group where you share outstanding books and novel ways of using them with students. Or get involved with a "Teacher As Reader" study group. Teachers need to get in touch with their own literacy behavior, if they hope to help their students develop into readers, writers, and learners.

Good luck!

REFERENCES

Aoki, M. E. (1981). Are you Chinese? Are you Japanese? Or are you just a mixed-up kid?—Using Asian American children's literature. *The Reading Teacher, 34*, 382–385.

Beane, J. A. (1993). *A middle school curriculum: From rhetoric to reality* (2nd ed.). Columbus, OH: National Middle School Association.

Benedict, S. (1992). Picture books let the imagination soar. In S. Benedict and L. Carlisle (Eds.), *Beyond words: Picture books for older readers and writers* (pp. 33–48). Portsmouth, NH: Heinemann.

Benson, D. (1991). Literature livens U.S. history. *The Colorado Communicator, 14*, 21.

Bishop, R. S., & Hickman, J. Four or fourteen or forty: Picture books are for everyone. In S. Benedict and L. Carlisle (Eds.), *Beyond words: Picture books for older readers and writers* (pp. 1–10). Portsmouth, NH: Heinemann.

Carlson, R.K. (1972). *Emerging humanity, multi-ethnic literature for children and adolescents.* Dubuque, IA: Brown.

Commission of Minority Participation in Education and American Life (CMPEAL). *One third of a nation.* Washington, D.C.: CMPEAL.

DeFord, D. (1981). Literacy: Reading, writing, and other essentials. *Language Arts, 58,* 652–658.

Dewey, J. (1933). *How we think* (rev. ed.). Boston, MA: Heath.

Drake, S.M. (1993). *Planning integrated curriculum: The call to adventure.* Alexandria, VA: Association for Supervision, Curriculum, and Development.

Eckhoff, B. (1983). How reading affects children's writing. *Language Arts,60,* 607–616.

Elleman, B. (1992). The nonfiction scene: What's happening? In E.B. Freeman and D.G. Person (Eds.), *Using Nonfiction Trade Books in the Elementary Classroom: From ants to zeppelins* (pp. 26–33). Urbana, IL: National Council of Teachers of English.

Fogarty, R. (1991). *The mindful school: How to integrate the curricula.* Pallantine, IL: Skylight Publishing.

Gagnon, P. (1989). *Democracy's half-told story.* Washington, D.C.: American Federation of Teachers.

Galda, L. (1993). Giving the gift of a poet's words: Sharing poetry with older children. *Fanfare: The Christopher-Gordon Children's Literature Annual, 1,* 105–116.

Hall, S. (1990). *Using picture storybooks to teach literary devices: Recommended books for children and young adults.* Phoenix, AZ: Oryx Press.

Hentoff, N. (1984, February). The duming of America. *The Progressive,* pp. 29–31.

Hickman, J., & Cullinan, B. E. (1989). A point of view on literature and learning. In J. Hickman and B.E. Cullinan (Eds.), *Children's literature in the classroom: Weaving Charlotte's Web* (pp. 3–12). Norwood, MA: Christopher-Gordon.

Huck, C. S. (1989). Epilogue: In the words of Charlotte S. Huck. In J. Hickman and B. E. Cullinan (Eds.), *Children's literature in the classroom: Weaving Charlotte's Web* (pp. 251–262). Norwood, MA: Christopher-Gordon.

Huck, C. S. (1982). I give you the end of a golden string. *Theory into Practice, 21,* 315–321.

Jacobs, H. H. (1989). *Interdisciplinary curriculum: Design and implementation*. Alexandria, VA: Association for Supervision, Curriculum, and Development.

Jenks, C. K. (1992). Invitation from the librarian: Picture books for older children. In S. Benedict and L. Carlisle (Eds.), *Beyond words: Picture books for older readers and writers* (pp.99–105). Portsmouth, NH: Heinemann.

Lipson, M. Y., Valencia, S. W., Wixson, K. K., & Peters, C. W. (1993). Integrating and thematic teaching: Integration to improve teaching and learning. *Language Arts, 70*, 252–263.

McClure, A., Harrison, P., & Reed, P. (1989). Poetry in the school: Bringing children and poetry together. In J. Hickman and B. E. Cullinan (Eds.), *Children's literature in the classroom: Weaving Charlotte's Web* (pp. 173–188). Norwood, MA: Christopher-Gordon.

McClure, A. A., with P. Harrison and Sheryl Reed. (1990). *Sunrises and songs: Reading and writing poetry in an elementary classroom*. Portsmouth, NH: Heinemann.

Mills, E. (1974). Children's literature and teaching written composition. *Elementary English, 51*, 971–973.

Norton, D. E. (1983). *Through the eyes of a child*. Columbus, OH: Charles E. Merrill.

Ramirez Jr., G. & Ramirez, J.L. (1994). *Multiethnic children's literature*. Albany, NY: Delmar Publishers.

Rasinski, T., & Padak, N.D. (1990). Multicultural learning through children's literature. *Language Arts, 67*, 576–580.

Reif, L. (1992). Good children's literature is for everyone, even especially adolescents. In S. Benedict and L. Carlisle (Eds.), *Beyond words: Picture books for older readers and writers* (pp. 69–87). Portsmouth, NH: Heinemann.

Siu-Runyan, Y. (1994). Interview with Rosemary Salesi: Why use nonfiction across the curriculum? *The Colorado Communicator, 17*, 4–11.

Stelk, V. (1989). Fantasy in the classroom. In J. Hickman and B. E. Cullinan (Eds.), *Children's literature in the classroom: Weaving Charlotte's Web* (pp. 121–127). Norwood, MA: Christopher-Gordon.

Stevenson, C., & Carr, J. (1993). *Integrated studies in the middle grades: Dancing through walls*. New York: Teacher College Press.

Tunnell, M. O., & Ammon, R. (1993). Introduction. In M. O. Tunnell and R. Ammon (Eds.) *The story of ourselves: Teaching history through children's literature* (p. vii). Portsmouth, NH: Heinemann.

Vars, G. F. (1987). *Interdisciplinary teaching in the middle grades.* Columbus, OH: National Middle School Association.

Woolsey, D. (1989). Fantasy literature for children. In J. Hickman and B. Cullinan (Eds.), *Children's literature in the classroom: Weaving Charlotte's Web* (pp. 109–119). Norwood, MA: Christopher-Gordon.

PROFESSIONAL BOOKS

Atwell, N. (Ed.). (1990). *Coming to know: Writing to learn in the intermediate grades.* Portsmouth, NH: Heinemann.

Atwell, N. (1987). *In the middle: Writing, reading, and learning with adolescents.* Portsmouth, NH: Heinemann.

Harwayne, S. (1992). *Lasting impressions: Weaving literature into the writing workshop.* Portsmouth, NH: Heinemann.

Harris, V. J. (Ed.). (1992). *Teaching multicultural literature in grades K–8.* Norwood, MA: Christopher-Gordon.

Moss, J. F. (1994). *Using literature in the middle grades: A thematic approach.* Norwood, MA: Christopher Gordon.

Reif, L. (1992). *Seeking diversity: Language arts with adolescents.* Portsmouth, NH: Heinemann.

LITERATURE RESOURCES

Benedict, S., & Carlisle, L., (Eds.). (1992). *Beyond words: Picture books for older readers and writers.* Portsmouth, NH: Heinemann.

Freeman, E. B., & Goetz, D. (Eds.). (1992). *Using nonfiction trade books in the elementary classroom: From ants to zeppelins.* Urbana, IL: National Council of Teachers of English.

Hall, S. (1990). *Using picture storybooks to teach literary devices: Recommended books for children and young adults.* Phoenix, AZ: Oryx Press.

Huck, C. S., Hepler, S., & Hickman, J. (1989). *Children's literature in the elementary school* (fifth edition). Orlando, FL: Harcourt Brace Jovanovich.

Jenson, J. M., & Roser, N. L. (Eds.). (1993). *Adventuring with books: A booklist for pre-K–Grade 6* (tenth edition). Urbana, IL: National Council of Teachers of English.

Moir, H., with M. Cain & L. Prosak-Beres. (Eds.). *Collected perspectives: Choosing and using books for the classroom* (second edition). Norwood, MA: Christopher-Gordon.

Ramirez Jr., G. & Ramirez, J.L. (1994). *Multiethnic children's literature.* Albany, NY: Delmar Publishers.

Saul, W., & Jagusch, S.A. (Eds.). (1991). *Vital connections: Children, science, and books.* Portsmouth, NH: Heinemann.

Tunnell, M. O., & Ammon, R. (Eds.). (1993). *The story of ourselves: Teaching history through children's literature.* Portsmouth, NH: Heinemann.

Webb, C.A. (Eds.). (1993). *Your reading: A booklist for junior high and middle school* (ninth edition). Urbana, IL: National Council of Teachers of English.

Literature Cited

Adler, C. S. (1991). *Mismatched summer.* G. P. Putnam's Sons.

Auch, M. J. (1992). *Out of step.* Holiday House.

Banks, L. R. (1991). *One more river.* Morrow Junior Books.

Barron, T. A. (1992). *The ancient one.* Philomel Books.

Brooks, B. (1992). *What hearts?* HarperCollins.

Bunting, E. (1980). *The terrible things.* Illustrated by Stephen Gammell. Philadelphia, NY: Jewish Publication Society.

Carkeet, D. (1991). *Quiver river.* HarperCollins.

Cannon, A. E. (1991). *Amazing Gracie.* Delacorte Press.

Chetwin, G. (1990). *Collidescope.* Bradbury Press.

Clement, C. (1989). *The voice of the wood.* Translated by Lenny Hort. Illustrated by Frederic Clement. Dial Books.

Coerr, E. (1993). *Sadako.* Illustrated by Ed Young. G. P. Putnam's Sons.

Dunning, S., Lueders, E., and Smith, H. (1966). *Reflections on a gift of a watermelon pickle and other modern verses.* Lothrop.

Garland, S. (1992). *Song of the buffalo boy.* Harcourt Brace Jovanovich.

George, J. C. (1987). *The talking earth.* HarperCollins.

Gogol, S. (1991). *Vatsana's lucky new year.* Lerner Publications Company.

Goldstein, B. S. (1992). *Inner chimes: Poems on poetry.* Illustrated by J. B. Breskim. Boyds Mills Press.

Greene, B. (1991). *The drowning of Stephan Jones.* Greenwillow Books.

Hahn, M. D. (1988). *December stillness.* Clarion Books.

Hamanaka, S. (1990). *The journey.* Illustrated by author. Orchard Books.

Heese, Karen. (1992). *Letters from Rifka.* Henry Holt.

Hamilton, V. (1967). *Zeely.* Illustrated by Symeon Shimin. Macmillan.

Janecsko, P. B. (1991). *Poetspeak: In their work, about their work.* Collier/Macmillan.

Janeczko, P. B. (1990). *The place my words are looking for.* Bradbury Press.

Hurwitz, J. (1990). *Class president.* Morrow Junior Books.

Johnson, E. R. (1992). *A house full of strangers.* Cobblehill Books.

Kronenwetter, M. (1992). *United they hate.* Walker and Company.

Lampman, E. S. (1976). *The potlatch family.* Atheneum.

Lehrman, R. (1990). *Separations.* Viking Penguin.

L'Engle, M. (1989). *An acceptable time.* Farrar, Straus, and Giroux.

Livingston, M. C. (1989). *Remembering and other poems.* Margaret K. McElderry Books.

Lowry, L. (1989). *Number the stars.* Houghton Mifflin.

Lowry, L. (1993). *The giver.* Houghton Mifflin.

Mayne, W. (1990). *Drift.* A Yearling Book.

Mori, K. (1993). *Shizuko's daughter.* Henry Holt.

Morimoto, J. (1987). *My Hiroshima.* Illustrated by author. Viking Children's Books.

Neville, E. C. (1991). *The China year.* HarperCollins.

Nye, N. S. (1992). *This same sky: A collection of poems from around the world.* Macmillan.

Oppenheim, S. L. (1992). *The lily cupboard.* Illustrated by Ronald Himler. HarperCollins.

Paulsen, G. (987). *Hachet.* Puffin Books.

Pettit, J. (1992). *My name is San Ho.* Scholastic.

Sherlock, P. (1991). *Four of a kind.* Holiday House.

Ray, D. K. (1990). *My Daddy was a soldier.* Illustrated by author. Holiday House.

Salisbury, G. (1992). *Blue skin of the sea.* Delacorte Press.

Salisbury;, G. (1994). *Under the blood-red sun.* Delacorte Press.

Soto, G. (1992). *Pacific crossing.* Harcourt Brace Jovanovich.

Soto, G. (1990). *A summer life.* Laurel-Leaf Books.

Steiber, E. (1992). *Eighth grade changes everything.* Troll Associates.

Tsuchiya, Y. (1988). *Faithful elephants: A true story of animals, people and war.* Translated by Tomoko Tsuchiya Dykes. Illustrated by Ted Lewin. Houghton Mifflin.

Uchida, Y. (1993). *The bracelet.* Illustrated by Joanna Yardley. Philomel.

Walter, M. P. (1992). *Mississippi challenge.* Bradbury Press.

Watkins, Y. K. (1986). *So far from the bamboo grove.* Lothrop, Lee & Shepard.

Wild, Margaret. (1991). *Let the celebrations begin!* Illustrated by Julie Vivas. Orchard Books.

Wolff, V. E. (1993). *Make lemonade*. Henry Holt.

Woodson, J. (1992). *Maizon at Blue Hill*. Delacorte Press.

Yep, L. (1977). *Child of the owl*. Harper & Row.

Yep, L. (1975). *Dragonwings*. Harper & Row.

Yep, L. (1991). *The star fisher*. Puffin Books.

CHAPTER 9

Helping Students Construct Big Understandings

Debbie Powell and Dick Needham

We recently attended a PTO meeting in which a group of parents asserted that children were not learning the basic skills or the content they would need to succeed in school or beyond. A very reflective and effective teacher responded, "We don't teach the subjects; we teach our students." This situation is typical of the polarization that occurs in our schools today over issues such as learner-centered vs. subject- or content-centered curriculum. Similar debates have occurred among educators and between educators and their publics for decades. John Dewey discussed this polarization in *Experience and Education* (1938):

> Mankind (sic) likes to think in terms of extreme opposites. It is given to formulating Either-Ors, between which it recognizes no intermediate possibilities.

This chapter focuses on the "intermediate possibilities" between the learner and what is to be learned in an integrated curriculum. We base our understandings of the need for and the possibilities of a balanced curriculum on our collaboration with middle and elementary level teachers through the Elementary Science Implementation (ESI) Project at the University of Northern Colorado. Through this four-year teacher enhancement program, funded by the National Science Foundation and the University of Northern Colorado, we were able to observe and learn how teachers engage students in their own investigations to construct personal and shared understandings of the physical and social world. We have inquired how teachers facilitate students' sharing and explaining of complex and abstract concepts. Most importantly, we've inquired how teachers assist learners in making connections between what they are learning and their own world.

Our position on the nature and function of curriculum and its relationship to the learner might be called "centerism," a term Martinello and Cook (1994, p. 3) use to describe the need for a balanced view. We believe our views are well-grounded in classroom research, whole language, and social constructivists' theories, and inquiry and are not a compromise of any of the beliefs we individually and collectively brought to the ESI Project.

Integration, as we define it, is primarily between the learners and their world, not merely between and among subject areas. The subject area connections should be as natural as they exist in the world. Hartoonian and Stock (1992) suggest that people live at the intersection of culture and environment. Although cultures are forged and modified by environment, there are cultural universals, elements common to all nations and people, that all nations and cultures share. It is important to understand our culture, if we are to understand our world and be effective citizens in our society and the global community. How we operate within this sociocultural system affects our immediate and global environment which, in turn, affects our culture. Our point is that the world is naturally integrated around science and the social sciences. One way to represent knowledge in the sciences, the social sciences and the intersection of the disciplines is through broad generalizations or statements we refer to as "big understandings."

Big understandings reflect patterns of human behavior and natural phenomena, or the interaction of humans in their physical environment. Big understandings focus on the knowledge which helps us understand ourselves and the world in which we live. Planning learning experiences around significant content such as this provides a means for adolescent learners to effectively utilize knowledge to inquire about and construct understandings about humans and their interactions in their physical and social world.

When we begin with a rich context of conceptual learning, students can learn significant content that has the potential to be life changing. At the same time, the multiple communication systems of language, mathematics, and the arts help us learn and communicate about our culture and environment. The interrelationship of content, process, and dispositions creates a natural integration. What students need to thrive and sometimes survive in their world today are the same skills and attitudes future employers want (U.S. Department of Labor, 1988): ability to learn, adaptability, creative thinking and problem-solving skills, effective communication skills, personal management, group effectiveness, and organizational effectiveness and leadership. We think that characteristics such as honesty and integrity, responsibility, compassion, self-discipline, fortitude, and respect for self and others are also important. These skills, processes, and personal characteristics don't occur in a vacuum outside of school, and they don't need to in school either. Significant content, processes, and dispositions can and should all be learned and taught simultaneously—the essence of an integrated curriculum.

As this book is published, many national committees, funded by the federal government and other agencies, are developing national standards for geography, history, economics, language arts, science, and foreign languages. The standards for mathematics and the arts are already published. The depth and breadth of these standards are overwhelming. Though these national standards are voluntary, many state curricula are mandated by law. In some schools, teachers also feel great pressure to follow district guidelines. Unlike most scope and sequences, the standards are chunked in large bands (e.g., grades 5-8). Currently, teachers at one grade level often have difficulty seeing the big picture—where learners have been and where they are going. Having a broad outline of the entire scope could be useful, but also very confusing to sort out just what is each individual's or team's responsibility. A well-developed curriculum based on big understandings can help teachers define parameters of classroom inquiry and be assured that they have been accountable for a necessary part of their students' education.

Teacher as Mediator of the Curriculum

Larry Spohn, a middle level science teacher, asks himself daily, "What is important for my students to learn?" Larry teaches science and is committed to helping his students think scientifically and understand the nature of science. Larry views his district-adopted textbook curriculum as only one way to represent the world, and he knows that he must mediate this curriculum among the students he teaches if he is going to facilitate their understanding of the world. Larry, like many teachers in the ESI Project, found that his students' interests mirror those critical issues and problems humans face in our complex world. These are mirrored also in the various draft statements of the national standards for science (National Committee on Science Education Standards and Assessment, May 1994) and the social sciences (e.g., National History Standards Project, March 1994; Geography for Life, October 1993). The role of the teacher, therefore, is to help students develop the shared knowledge and understandings that make up our cultures and to help develop the meaning and relevance that can affect students' lives and understandings of their own culture.

Developing big understandings is one way to mediate the curriculum with students' prior experiences and knowledge. If you are a member of an integrated team, you can share a big understanding that all subject area teachers work toward. Within this broad generalization, you and the students can plan inquiry that engages your students. If you are teaching a single subject, you will begin seeing connections to other subject areas, but more importantly, you will be able to help children see connections between what they are learning in school and their lives.

Many middle level teachers consider themselves content teachers and want their students to understand and appreciate their particular subject area. There are, however, three questions we've found critical for teachers to answer in planning and negotiating the curriculum. We will address these three questions to help you use them as guides in your own planning:

1.   What is important for my students to understand and why?

2.   How can I organize and frame this content so my students will perceive it as important for them to know and understand?

3.   How will I know if my students have these understandings?

The first question, "What is important for my students to understand and why?" often initially leads to a laundry list of facts, concepts, and sometimes generalizations. We've observed that when teachers go the next step to ask themselves why this is important, their responses range from the immediate and practical concerns regarding assessment of goals or outcomes to broader considerations regarding going to college and gaining employment. Teachers are wise to consider all of these.

Middle school students, however, need educational experiences that address life today as well as in the future. As Dewey pointed out, we can't forget that these individuals' lives don't begin when they leave school—they *are* citizens in a pluralistic, ever-changing environment *now*. When teachers can answer the question, "Why is this important for my students to know and understand?" in a way that relates to the student's world outside of school, they are more likely to affect these young people's lives significantly. They're more likely to engage students effectively in learning. What's important to teach is not only what's essential from a teacher and content perspective, but also from a learner's perspective. Our curriculum should derive from *both* important generalizations and key concepts and the learners' needs and interests. These broad generalizations linked to the students' worlds are what we refer to as big understandings. The challenge becomes being able to set up the context and learning situations and environments where students have a need to know what you know they will need.

The final question, "How will I know if my students have these under-standings?" relates to evaluation. Obviously, it is much easier to evaluate learning if you know *what* you are evaluating. We will offer some general suggestions that teachers in the ESI Project use when evaluating students' understanding.

What Is a Big Understanding?

The easiest way to think about big understandings is to ask yourself or your teammates, "If we had to say one thing that we want our students to walk away with from this unit, what would it be?" Now write this as a statement. Because a sentence is a complete thought by definition, you are connecting the concepts and ideas. *A big understanding is a single sentence that states the generalization you want your students to construct—to own.* We think a big understanding should represent broad generalizations that connect significant content with the learner's back-ground experiences and prior knowledge. We are not trying to teach the generalization or statement to the students; rather, we expect that generali-zations students draw by the end of the unit will mirror this statement. Teachers and students may generate statements that describe the social and physical world, such as the ones below.

- When we work together, we can effect changes in our govern-ment and country.

- Living things can adapt to hostile climates.

- Survival of an individual or group may require creative problem solving to overcome challenging situations.

- People migrate or move and settle for many different reasons.

- All humans have the same basic needs, but our values determine our "wants."

- Our community is constantly changing over time due to natural and cultural forces and processes, but sometimes people struggle to keep what they value.

- The existence of human beings represents a minute period in the ages of the earth's history.

- Living things either adapt to change or become extinct.

- Humans develop complex machines to solve life problems and to make their work more efficient.

- Choices made by individuals can bring about either negative or positive changes in our environment.

Teachers use the big understandings as a filter through which activities, resources, and learning experiences are selected or developed. There is no right or wrong when writing big understandings. The newly developed national standards (and/or state standards) may offer some assistance in selecting understandings that can be modified to meet the needs of your students. The guiding generalization may change in the course of co-creating and negotiating the curriculum with your students. You will also know how much freedom to allow students when making choices and when to provide them with more direction and guidance.

HOW ARE BIG UNDERSTANDINGS DIFFERENT FROM CONCEPTUAL THEMES OR TOPICS?

Often the thematic and topical units and the units developed around big understandings aren't that different in regard to the types of activities or the resources used. However, we believe that when teachers plan curriculum around a big understanding, they find it easier to create a meaningful context to link the range of understandings and processes in a meaningful and authentic way. In the limited time available in schools, teachers can challenge learners with significant content while they also teach processes in context and develop children's affect. The diversions and spontaneous activities can still occur, but the difference is that the teachers know when to pull the kids back in and when they may just need to change directions in the unit and even change the big understanding.

Beginning with a big understanding provides a target for what you want students to construct and suggests outcomes in terms of application of the understanding. It is a broad and overarching target, however, not narrow and limiting. Planning around a big understanding provides a screen to help you know which questions to ask in investigations and in group decision-making activities and which experiments, simulations, role plays, and other activities will best help students construct what you know they need to know.

WRITING BIG UNDERSTANDINGS

There are many ways to develop big understandings. Debbie begins by surrounding herself with resources on the topic. She feels that she needs to be more comfortable with the content before she begins thinking about concepts or generalizations. Dick begins by developing a concept web because he feels he has a grasp of the information and concepts.

Both are good ideas, and we eventually do both, regardless of how we begin the planning process. Writing big understandings is much easier with a teaching partner. We usually brainstorm a web together (Debbie with the resources in front on her and Dick with the pencil and paper). This web is usually very broad and could be a year-long unit. This phase is important, however, to put our unit in a bigger context.

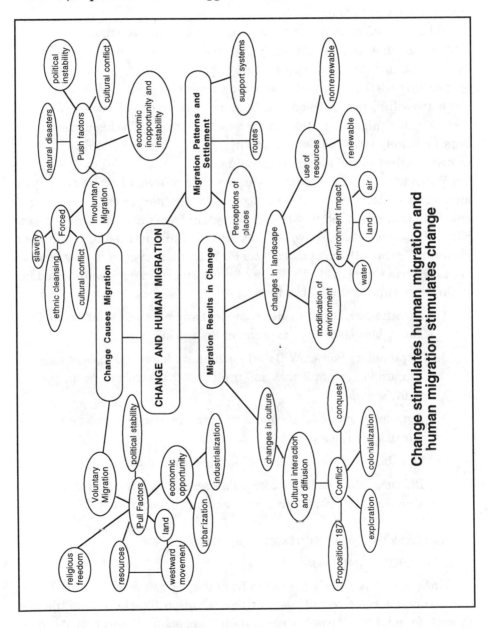

Figure 9.1

Next, we write the understanding and then re-web, focusing in on the concepts that link to our big understanding. We ask ourselves, "What is significant for these learners to learn about this topic?" We are trying to help connect learners with their world, so we are always conscious of this question. Many people try to make planning a step-by-step process neat and clean, It is not! We find that for most teachers, planning is very organic and varies from unit to unit.

When one of us is very familiar with the content, we might begin with writing the big understanding. Some teachers begin with activities or resources that they know and then work the other direction in their planning to come up with the understanding and concepts being taught. This can work if you are willing to then re-adjust the activities that don't fit when you have decided the significant content learners will construct. The big understanding should help you decide which activities best fit. The two should be closely linked—activities and big understandings.

When working with a team of teachers from different subject areas, you may agree to develop the initial concept web together. In this way you are able to help one another view the same content from different perspectives. Hilda Taba and others have written about planning around significant content. We think that Taba's criteria for main ideas (which is very similar to the criteria stated in 2061's *Science for All Americans*) are well-suited for evaluating your big understandings.

1. Significance. Does the idea represent an important relationship about some aspect (or aspects) of the world?

2. Explanatory Power. Will the idea help students understand and explain important issues and problems that confront people in today's world?

3. Appropriateness. Is the idea suited to the needs, interests, and maturity of the students?

4. Durability. Is the idea one of lasting importance?

5. Balance. Will the idea promote a breadth and depth of understanding of events, individuals, actions, or occurrences?

How Can You Effectively Assess Big Understandings?

Knowing what you are assessing from the beginning of the unit guides the nature of formative and summative evaluation. Teachers from the ESI Project found it much easier to plan their on-going unit assessments when they began with a big understanding. The big understanding encompasses numerous concepts that are developed to form the bigger generalization. Knowing this at the beginning of the unit enables teachers to asses these concepts and to engage or re-engage students in investigations to construct their own understandings. As students share their generalizations, teachers may need to clarify concepts and add vocabulary terms to new understandings. Students can compare their generalizations as well as build on each others' explanations. This helps students not only know what they know, but what others know also.

Teachers in the ESI Project have relied on the wealth of literature on performance, portfolio, and authentic assessment (e.g., Tierney, *et al.*, 1991; Hill & Ruptic, 1994; Hein, 1990; and Harp, 1991). In their formative assessment, teachers use writing, drawing, and hands-on demonstrations supported by students' verbal explanations to assess concept development. Teachers have created multiple ways to gather evidence from these experiences to put into students' portfolios. Because the big understanding is connected to the students' world, students' projects, performances, and products at the end of the unit are a reflection of their understandings and are a major source for summative assessments. Teachers often use criteria arranged in a rubric to evaluate the unit projects. Demonstration of the big understanding would be one of these criteria.

Students demonstrate their understandings not only through the connections they make in their actual projects, but also by what they say and write. We use small-group work as one way to evaluate the learning that has occurred. It is often when students hear other students discuss what they know that they add a missing piece to their big picture and see a broader generalization. We think this is important and often produces richer explanations. This alone, however, is not enough. We often ask students to individually write one or two sentences summarizing what they have learned from all of their experiences in the unit. We also ask them to sit with us and explain their projects, why they made the generalizations they did. We discuss or ask them to write or draw about connections they are making between their big understanding and their daily lives. When teachers know a target for learning, they can be assessing how close students are coming to that target and how to structure the environment where all students eventually hit that target. At the same time, they will be constructing shared understandings—the basis of culture and cooperation.

In Summary

As one teacher said about the process of planning integrated units around big understandings, "It is almost so simple it is hard. I have gained an understanding of how critical it is to have a framework. It has given purpose to my teaching of the content and has allowed me to see the big picture." The scores of teachers we have worked with are now asking themselves, "So what's my big understanding and how can I make this content relevant to my students' lives?" They find that they can be true to their whole language, inquiry, or guided discovery philosophies and still meet the guidelines of their district or state curriculum. They feel that they are being accountable for their share of the total curriculum.

REFERENCES

Dewey, J. (1916). *Democracy and education*. New York, NY: Macmillan.

Dewey, J. (1933). *How we think*. Boston: D. C. Heath.

Dewey, J. (1938). *Experience & education*. New York, NY: Collier.

Harp, B. (Ed.). (1991). *Assessment and evaluation in whole language programs*. Norwood, MA: Christopher-Gordon Publishers, Inc.

Hartoonian, H. M., & Stock, H. (1992). *A guide to curriculum planning in global studies*. Madison, WI: Wisconsin Department of Public Instruction.

Hill, B. C., & Ruptic, C. (1994). *Practical aspects of authentic assessment: Putting the pieces together*. Norwood, MA: Christopher-Gordon Publishers, Inc.

Martinello, M., & Gillian, C. (1994). *Interdisciplinary inquiry in teaching and learning*. New York, NY: Merrill.

Taba, H. (1971). *Teachers handbook for elementary social studies*. Reading, MA: Addison Wesley.

Tierney, R. J., Carter, M. A. & Desai, L. E. (1991). *Portfolio assessment in the reading-writing classroom*. Norwood, MA: Christopher Gordon Publishers, Inc.

U. S. Department of Labor (1988). *Workplace basics: The skills employers want*. Washington, D.C.: American Society for Training and Development.

CHAPTER 10

Service Learning and Middle School Students: The Perfect Fit

Elaine Andrus

At Panorama Middle School in Colorado Springs, Colorado, a team of ninety seventh-grade students have "adopted" thirty senior citizens who are transported to the school on a regular basis during the entire school year. This seventh-grade team, comprised of both students and teachers, has determined that an ongoing theme of community and citizenship would be enhanced by having the students develop relationships and use real-life skills through their contacts with their "adopted grandparent." After having explored the issue of aging in American society, role-playing what it is like to be elderly, word-processing a letter to their senior citizen, and many telephone conversations, students are eager as the big day arrives. The senior citizens are transported to the school by adult volunteers from the community. Smiles, tears, gifts, and lively conversations are exchanged throughout the four-hour school visit. Interviews are videotaped, and a deeper understanding of the history of the community has come alive. As one student explains, "Our team's service learning experience opens up the heart of our school and makes learning real."

Marian Wright Edelman (1992) states in her book *The Measure of Our Success—a Letter to My Children and Yours:*

> "Diverse opportunities for young people to serve their communities can play a major role in restoring hope and moral example to our nation. Young people need to believe they are needed, and adults need to be reminded that our

children and youth all have something to contribute and are precious resources to be nurtured and cherished" (p. 67).

Service learning is a teaching and learning strategy which recognizes the demonstrated positive and altruistic qualities of our youth, providing opportunities for young people to exert their leadership skills and to apply what is learned in the classroom to a real-life setting. Through service learning opportunities, society will view young people as "producers and givers" rather than the stereotype of "receivers or takers." This is an important step in unleashing the potential of youth as well as making learning relevant.

The advent of service learning as a teaching and learning strategy promotes curriculum integration, is an authentic assessment process, and is the "intersection of personal concerns and social issues" for early adolescents, which James A. Beane (1993) describes in his book, *Middle School Curriculum, From Rhetoric to Reality,* (2nd ed.). Below, Beane's original chart which provides sample intersections of personal and social concerns, has been slightly revised in order to show how service learning fits with middle level students' personal and social concerns.

Figure 10-1
(Sample) Intersections of Personal and Social Concerns by James Beane
expanded with Examples of Service Learning Activities

EARLY ADOLESCENT CONCERNS	CURRICULUM THEMES	SOCIAL CONCERNS	SERVICE LEARNING ACTIVITIES
Understanding personal changes	TRANSITIONS	Living in a changing world	Adopt senior citizen grandparents; develop a latch-key program for elementary students
Developing a personal identity	IDENTITIES	Cultural diversity	Organize and present a community Martin Luther King Celebration and Black History Awareness series; prepare a videotaope and booklet about their neighborhood cultures

Finding a place in the group	INTERDEPENDENCE	Global interdependence	Become sharing pen pals with students from former communist countries; prepare friendship boxes for children in disaster areas around the world
Personal Fitness	WELLNESS	Environmental protection	Participate in National River Watch programs; serve as park volunteers; plant a community garden
Social status (e.g. among peers)	SOCIAL STRUCTURES	Class systems (by age, economics, etc.)	Adopt a homeless shelter; develop and implement plans for reducing hunger in the community
Dealing with adults	INDEPENDENCE	Human rights	Share recreational time with disabled children; survey youth about needs, and adopt legislatures
Peer conflicts and gangs	CONFLICT RESOLUTION	Global conflict	Develop peer mediation and counseling program; develop and present drug awareness program
Commercial pressures	COMMERCIALISM	Effects of media	Serve as consumer watchdogs; conduct comparison studies of food prices
Questioning authority	JUSTICE	Laws and social customs	Track and publish voting records of public officials; get community members to vote
Personal friendships	CARING	Social welfare	Participate in special olympics; adopt headstart preschool buddies
Living in the school	INSTITUTIONS	Social institutions	Prepare a transition program for 5th graders moving to middle school; adopt a hospital or Ronald McDonald house

What Is Service Learning?

The National and Community Service Act of 1990 (Learn and Serve America, 1994) states that service learning is a method:

- under which students learn and develop through active participation in thoughtfully organized service experiences that meet actual community needs and that are coordinated in collaboration with the school and community;

- that is integrated into students' academic curriculum and provides structured time for students to think, talk, or write about what they did and said during the actual service activity;

- that provides students with the opportunities to use newly acquired skills and knowledge in real life situations in their own communities;

- that enhances what is taught in school by extending student learning beyond the classroom and into the community and helps foster the development of a sense of caring for others.

In other words, service learning as a teaching and learning strategy goes *beyond* doing community service. Community service projects are doing isolated "acts of kindness," such as supporting canned food drives, hosting a school recycling day, or having the school choir sing at a senior citizen community center. Service learning is more than "acts of kindness." Service learning enables young people to use what is learned in classrooms and apply that knowledge and generalized learning to real-life situations and problems, followed by a formal reflection component.

For teachers, service learning is a way of teaching, which changes the role of the teacher from a giver of knowledge to a facilitator of learning. The teacher is a coach who provides students with active/reflective experiential learning experiences. Hands-on first-hand learning is, of course, appropriate to the developmental needs of early adolescents (see Chapter 1 by Brazee).

Service learning also forms a natural bridge between schools, parents, and communities. The African proverb "It takes a whole village to raise a child" is excellent advice for a society of disjointed communities, non-traditional families, and large number of young people in at-risk environments. In addition, for service learning to work, community agencies must be appreciated as important educational resources and integrated partners in the planning, implementation, and evaluation of service learning opportunities. Thus, joint in-service opportunities must be available for both school and community collaborators.

Through this collaborative venture between schools and the community, many positive outcomes are achieved for educators, schools, and communities in the following ways.

Students learn:

- leadership skills—empowerment of others and self
- growth of self-esteem and a positive self-concept, a sense that they can and do make a difference
- citizenship skills through actual experience—responsibility to self, school, family, community, country, and world
- improved academic skills—critical thinking and creative problem-solving applications of learning to real-life
- career awareness and exploration
- opportunities to become connected with people of all ages, diversities, backgrounds, and needs

Educators gain:

- students motivated to learn
- opportunities for professional development
- positive connections to community and parents
- an important teaching strategy which integrates curriculum and provides experiential, hands-on learning for students
- an effective method for authentic assessment
- empowerment

Schools develop:

- engaged, motivated learners who are responsible for their learning
- better student attendance rates and less discipline problems;
- higher academic achievement
- connections with community, parents, higher education, and business
- integrated curriculum, authentic assessment, a climate of caring
- positive public opinion and recognition

Communities receive:

- valuable service to meet needs

- engaged, responsible citizens

- an infusion of creativity and enthusiasm from participating youth

- collaborative partnerships to focus on building community

Ernest L. Boyer (1983) states:
> "During our study of the nation's schools, I became convinced that the problems of our schools are inextricably tied to this larger problem—the feeling on the part of many of our youth that they are isolated, unconnected to the larger world outside their classrooms. Again and again during our study, we met young people who saw little, if any, connection between what they were doing and learning in school and communities in which they lived... To encourage young people to become more fully involved in their communities, we proposed in High School that every student complete a service requirement—a new "Carnegie unit" that would involve them in volunteer work in the community or at school... I believe such a service program taps an enormous source of talent, lets young people know that they are needed, and helps students see a connection between what they learn and how they live" (p. 7).

In other words, the key to transforming student apathy into student engagement is to *allow students to make decisions about their learning*. To be sure, there is nothing new about the idea that students should be able to participate, individually and collectively, in making decisions. This conviction has long played a role in schools designated as progressive, democratic, open, free, experimental, or alternative. In educational philosophies, this kind of student involvement is called developmental, constructivist, holistic, or learner-centered. In specific innovations, they are referred to as whole-language, discovery-based science, cooperative learning, or authentic assessment. So, service learning can be defined as a teaching and learning strategy which empowers adolescents not only to develop intellectually, but also to learn to become responsible, caring persons who can make good choices and solve problems effectively (Boyer 1987).

Funding for Service Learning

The 1990 National and Community Service Act provided $16 million in funding in 1992 and 1993 to fuel service learning nationwide through its K–12 Serve-America School and Community-based allocation. Through The National and Community Service Trust Act of 1993, this legacy has been practically doubled to $30 million for the years 1994, 1995, and 1996, through the Learn and Serve America K–12 funding stream. The Corporation for National and Community Service has been established in Washington D.C. to make allocations through state education agencies with direct support to individual teachers, teacher teams, schools, school districts, and community agencies.

In order to be funded, school-based service learning opportunities must engage elementary, middle, and high school students of different ages, races, genders, ethnic groups, disabilities, or economic backgrounds in a variety of service learning activities. These student service learning activities must promote academic and personal growth and at the same time, address the community's unmet human, educational, environmental, and public safety needs (Learn and Serve America, 1994).

Service Learning and Educational Reform

Learning through service is an idea that is bubbling up, rather than trickling down. Fueled by a fresh infusion of energy during the 1980s, it rekindles an idea brought to life by John Dewey in the 1930s—that schools should be democratic laboratories of learning, closely linked to community needs. These learning labs create new roles for students and teachers, make use of action-based instructional methods, and lead to the learning of meaningful, real-world content (Nathan and Kielsmeier, 1991).

In the wake of the 1980s wave of school reform, stimulated by the National Commission on Excellence in Education's 1983 release of "A Nation at Risk," nearly every state in the U.S. has some form of legislation for improving schools. Service learning is seen not as a separate reform effort, but an important component of several educational restructuring efforts.

GOALS 2000

On March 31, 1994, President Clinton signed into law "Goals 2000: Educate America Act." The purpose of the Act is to encourage higher levels of learning among all students and improve teaching for an increasingly diverse student population. Service learning has direct relevance to the following: Goal Three—School Achievement and Citizenship; Goal Seven— Safe, Disciplined and Alcohol and Drug-Free Schools; and Goal Eight—

Parental Participation. Service learning is also a teaching and learning strategy which will have an effect on: Goal Two—School Completion; Goal Three—Teacher Education and Professional Development; and Goal Six—Adult Literacy and Lifelong Learning. Goal One—School Readiness—can be achieved through the implementation of cross-age tutoring between middle school students and preschoolers as well as community literacy projects sponsored by a middle school team of teachers and students.

SCHOOL-TO-WORK

School-to-Work legislation, entitled the "Carl D. Perkins Vocational and Applied Technology Education Act," also includes service learning as an important component. School-to-Work means, "...Such programs shall include competency-based applied learning that contributes to an individual's academic knowledge, higher-order reasoning, problem-solving skills, work attitudes, general employable skills, and the occupational-specific skills necessary for economic independence as a productive and contributing member of society. Furthermore, vocational education services and activities described in Title II may include programs that involve students in addressing the needs of the community in the production of goods or services that contribute to the community's welfare or that involve the students with other community development planning, institutions, and enterprises. In addition, academic credit may be granted for vocational education courses that integrate core academic competencies" (Carl D. Perkins Vocational and Applied Technology Education Act, Administrative Provisions, Title V, Part B). Effective School-to-Work programs include service learning as a technique: (1) to help students explore different careers through mentorship/service learning opportunities; (2) to make connections with the community as a resource to involve students with community problem-solving; and (3) to involve students in addressing the needs of their communities by providing desired goods and services.

TURNING POINTS

In 1989, the Carnegie Corporation launched a major initiative in middle grades reform entitled "Turning Points, Preparing American Youth for the 21st Century." The rationale for focusing on this level was that "...early adolescence offers opportunities to choose a path toward a productive and fulfilling life, and for many their last best chance to avoid a diminished future" (Carnegie Council of Adolescent Development, 1989). The report called for the transformation of middle schools to enable every middle school student to become an intellectually reflective person; a person enroute to a lifetime of meaningful work; a good citizen; a caring and ethical individual; and a healthy person. Service learning is a teaching and learning strategy which embodies all five of these characteristics associated with being an effective human being.

Integrating the most current research knowledge with considered and wise practice, the Carnegie Task Force on Education of Young Adolescents found that the transformation of education for young adolescents involves the following eight recommendations—all of which are enhanced through the implementation of service learning opportunities:

- *Create small communities for learning.* The structure of the middle school supports service learning through team organization and advisor-advisee programs. Service learning will promote team unity, bonding, and a humane focus throughout the year.

- *Teach a core academic program.* An integrated curriculum supports active learning and teaches young adolescents to be active citizens. These are major focuses of service learning.

- *Ensuring success for all students.* Service learning enables *all* students to feel connected and provides a breadth of opportunities for students of all abilities and interests.

- *Empower teachers and administrators with local governance.* Flexible block scheduling creates larger blocks of time for young people to be involved in service learning opportunities. Service learning programs are school-based and fit well with empowering local school staffs to be creative in planning service experiences unique to the school and community.

- *Teachers in middle grade schools should be selected and specially educated to teach young adolescents.* Service learning should be a teaching and learning strategy explored and experienced in curricular methods courses, as well as in all middle level education courses.

- *Improving academic performance through better health and fitness.* Service learning is a proactive preventative approach to promote healthy lifestyles. It provides community involvement in the educational process and thus helps to promote a more caring school community. Also, because students have responsibility for learning based on goal setting and choices, a sense of student efficacy is fostered, and the holistic development of youth is stressed.

- *Re-engaging families in the education of young adolescents.* Families can become actively involved in service learning activities *with* their children. They are the necessary connectors to the community.

- *Connecting schools with communities.* Placing students in youth service is a major focus of this recommendation. The connections to community become reciprocal—young people serve in the community and the community becomes more visible in the school.

Turning Points has provided a foundation for middle level reform, and service learning complements and strengthens the effectiveness of each recommendation.

STANDARDS-BASED EDUCATION

Student and school performance standards with authentic and portfolio assessment measures are being developed by many states. This critical move away from reliance on standardized achievement tests to describe progress will be a significant step forward in assessing student learning through performance-based outcomes. Examples of how service learning is being used for assessing standards are:

- Including service learning experiences in the student's portfolio which demonstrate knowledge and application of skills;

- Using service learning to generate extended learning products which demonstrate achievement of content standards;

- Testing students, using the service learning experiences as the content of the test, for basic skills in reading, writing, mathematics, social science, and sciences;

- Developing the philosophy and values of the curriculum standards by relating the service learning values of caring, social conscience, and citizenship;

- Improving the quality of instruction through service learning, which offers integrated learning opportunities, critical thinking, more meaningful learning, and opportunities for cooperative learning.

RE: LEARNING AND ESSENTIAL SCHOOLS REFORM

The Coalition of Essential Schools is a privately funded, semi-autonomous unit at Brown University. Established by Theodore Sizer in 1984, the Coalition espouses nine Common Principles which, taken together, challenge many traditional assumptions and practices of American schooling. The work of the Coalition focuses on research, outreach, and professional development activities to support and extend essential school practice. "Re: Learning" began in 1988 as a joint initiative of the Coalition for Essential Schools and the Education of the States to help the full spectrum of educators and policy makers—from schoolhouse to statehouse—who are interested in reforming their education systems. The goal of "Re: Learning" is to encourage thoughtful local redesign of classroom practices and of district administrative policies that support all students to learn to use their minds well.

A major connection from "Re: Learning" to service learning is the outcome evaluation process which is called "exhibitions." Exhibitions are described by Sizer (1989) as "the demonstration by a student that he or she understands a rich core of subject matter and, equally important, can use it in resourceful, persuasive and imaginative ways" (p. 54). The "tuning" or evaluation of the exhibition involves an assessment of: (1) the vision; (2) the assignment; (3) the level of support and coaching; (4) samples of work in progress as well as benchmark performances; and (5) previously agreed criteria for judging. Service learning provides an ideal opportunity for students to demonstrate their ability to apply their knowledge to real world situations in "resourceful, persuasive, and imaginative methods."

Service Learning is connected to the Nine Common Principles of "Re: Learning" in the following ways:

- Principle 1—Providing a context for the exhibition and evaluation of the application of knowledge and skills to the real world outside of school, showing that students can "use their minds well"

- Principle 2—Assisting each student in defining and mastering a limited set of essential skills through interaction with service professionals outside of schools

- Principle 3—Providing service learning opportunities to all students accommodating all abilities and interests

- Principle 4—Personalizing the service learning experiences to each students' interests and set of essential skills

- Principle 5—Carrying the "student-as-worker" model from the school to the community through service projects

- Principle 6—Demonstrating mastery of knowledge and skills in service learning settings as part of qualifying for a diploma

- Principle 7—Building values of mutual respect, trust, and decency through giving of one's self in service to the community. Service learning promotes family involvement in the school

- Principle 8—Reinforcing the role of educators as generalists by having staff involved in a variety of integrated service learning experiences;

- Principle 9—Involving community members in the service learning opportunities of students by having them take on the role of "coach." This will reduce coach-to-student ratios and also give students varied experiences when working with adults.

The preceding reform efforts were discussed because they are the least prescriptive and most likely to sustain a long-term commitment to change and renewal. Their connections to middle level reform are clearly evident and demonstrate the importance of infusing service learning as a teaching and learning strategy for *all* young adolescents.

Organizing Quality Service Learning Experiences: The "Nuts and Bolts"

Service learning opportunities must be well-planned and coordinated. There are four components necessary to implement quality experiences: (1) preparation; (2) involving students in meaningful integrated service learning experiences; (3) student reflection; and (4) evaluation of service learning projects and self-study.

PREPARATION

Preparation for service learning encompasses three major phases—collaborative building among participants, staff development, and student readiness. Collaborative building can be facilitated by establishing a school/community service learning action team to explore and implement service learning opportunities. An integrated strategic action plan needs to be created to focus efforts and to assure total participation. Members of this team should consist of: (1) educators, students, key community agencies, such as United Way, Parks and Recreation Services, hospitals, etc.; (2) adult service club representatives, such as Rotary, Junior League, Lions Club, etc.; and (3) higher education representatives, businesses, foundations, parents, school district office representatives, and other key players in the community. This team will not only provide the foundation and support for the establishment of service learning opportunities, but also promote an awareness and understanding of service learning as a teaching and learning strategy.

Staff development for the implementation of service learning needs to extend over time and to include presentation, demonstration, practice, and feedback on the essential components. Ongoing technical assistance, networking opportunities, active administrative leadership, study groups, and shared responsibility and decision-making will maintain the momentum.

Another kind of essential preparation involves the students themselves. Student preparation is crucial for achieving success, but there is no formula to determine exactly the right amount of preparation needed. It is usually better to err on the side of having done more than enough preparation, rather than not having done enough. The following suggested steps will help make the service learning more meaningful for middle school students:

- Build cohesion within the group. Members of a cohesive team know and respect each other.

- Clarify responsibilities and expectations.

- Explore service options so all young adolescents can make an informed decision on their participation. Student input is crucial in building leadership skills and the feeling of efficacy.

- Encourage students to become "community detectives" by surveying the community with a needs assessment to find out their options.

- Once a project has been decided upon, arouse interest in and commitment to the project. A site visit with an opportunity for a question/answer period with employees and clients would be optimal.

- Assess the knowledge and skills of each young person. This builds the confidence level of each individual. An integrated curriculum, basic skills instruction, and role-playing can enhance the effectiveness of experience.

- Develop background information about the people, site, and possible challenges the students may encounter. The goal is to sensitize and revise preconceptions.

- Develop and practice skills that will be helpful, from using a computer to listening to a senior citizen or a child. This should include practice in the skills needed to learn from service—to be vigilant observers and persistent questioners of the experience (Conrad & Hedin, 1987).

MEANINGFUL INTEGRATED SERVICE LEARNING EXPERIENCES

Service learning can take on many forms in schools. It can range from an isolated club activity which has low curriculum infusion to a community service class, a long-term community project, a school-wide theme activity, an instructional method in core curriculum, or finally to school-wide infusion as an educational reform strategy.

For example, as a class activity, a middle school team might adopt second graders and go on field trips to community agencies together and then do a whole language activity. The primary-grade "buddies" could tell their stories about the trips to the older students, who could write them down. The younger students might illustrate the stories they dictated to the older students. Together, they have their own meaningful books made and published.

As a school-wide theme project, "growing older" might be a focus. Sixth graders could adopt grandparents from the community, visit them, and write to them frequently. Seventh graders could develop oral histories and help the senior citizens with writing letters, raking leaves, going grocery shopping, and even reading to them. In a service learning project like this, not only would all students learn about aging, but their involvement would make their content learning more relevant and interesting.

Service learning can also be used as a base for an integrated curriculum. In one community, students work with government agencies monitoring the pollution in a local river as an activity for their ecology unit. Because students want to find answers to questions like: How do we determine what the pollution level(s) are? What factors affect the level of pollution? What kinds of positive actions can we take to lower significantly the level of pollution? and report the findings to others, the project combines many subject areas. These include: *science and math instruction,* (understanding pollution and environmental issues, calculating quantities of chemicals and graphing results); *language arts* (vocabulary, political cartooning, writing newspaper articles, letters, and reports); *art* (illustrating the reports, making posters for community awareness), and *social studies* (researching the history of the river and region and with a business partnership, constructing a historical walkway along the river). In this example, the service activity becomes the core of the learning objectives. In the most comprehensive use of service learning, all integrated themes and skill learning are related to the community and become authentic tasks for assessing the learning of each student.

Another example: Students can use and apply their foreign language instruction by serving as translators for non-English speaking community residents, perhaps through community social service agencies or hospitals. Or they could design a brochure of their community aimed at various populations and written in both English and Spanish. Putting together such a brochure would use social studies, language arts, art, and math skills all in the same project.

REFLECTION

Reflection is the process of gaining meaning and understanding from experience. Research indicates that thoughtfully planned reflection is key to successful experienced-based programs. Time must be set aside after each service learning experience for discussion and sharing—recalling what happened, who participated, and what each person accomplished. Anticipated and unanticipated learning are identified, as well as the exploration of feelings. The discussion of what skills and academic subject matter helped with planning and implementation of the experience is important to show the relationship of what is learned in the classroom and the application to real life.

Reflection, then, helps students to identify their own values, assess personal skills, develop empathy for others, and compare their assumptions about themselves, other individuals, groups, and organizations to real world experience. Young people are challenged to answer:

- What happened to me?
- What difference did I make?
- What does this experience mean for me? For my community?
- What have I learned and how does this learning relate to the academic areas I am studying?

EVALUATION AND SELF-STUDY

Constant evaluation and self-study must be a major component of quality service learning experiences. Not only should student assessment be documented but also community outcomes. Student assessment is necessary to measure the extent and quality of learning and if educational standards have been achieved. Important questions to ask in developing student assessments include:

- What skills, concepts, verbal information, and attitudes arc students to develop?
- What kinds of behavior demonstrate accomplishment of learner standards? Can students apply what they learned in new situations?
- To what extent do students use previous learning in new or similar situations?

- What kinds of challenges or situations should students be able to handle as a result of their experiences in service learning?

- What methods are effective in demonstrating accomplishments?

- Do students exhibit an increased sense of social responsibility, caring, efficacy, and an understanding of the issues based on research and study of background and history?

Types of Student Assessment:

- Attendance and/or job performance

- Learning logs document evidence of reflection on ways subject matter helped solve problems. Also, document the results of the service effort itself by including letters, photos, and test materials

- Level of student participation in discussions and choices for further study

- Development of products (artistic expressions, written reports, journals, etc.)

- Creative problem-solving

- Community assessment of student participation

Methods to document community outcomes include:

- Record and tally total hours served

- Record all service achieved

- Collect student products, including videos, reports, stories, photos

- Interview community members about the value of service to them

- Ask community contacts to complete a group assessment form

- Solicit letters of support from community leaders or from people or agencies served

- Clip newspaper articles and tape radio or TV coverage

The Challenges

In the implementation of service learning opportunities, the following challenges need to be addressed: scheduling, funding, liability issues, transportation, and staff commitment.

Scheduling. A middle level school which has flexible block scheduling and no passing bells possesses large blocks of time when service learning activities can be scheduled. The teaming concept allows flexibility for student involvement which can be integrated into regular class instruction and time. Advisor/advisee periods can also be utilized for in-school service learning activities.

Funding. Service learning can be funded through many sources including:

- Learn and Serve America federal grants allocated through state education agencies
- State legislative support where applicable
- Foundation grants
- Issue oriented funding such as drug-free school money, at risk youth, school-to-work transition, etc.
- Service Club Partnerships - Rotary, Kiwanis, Lions (which provides Quest training across the nation, including a service learning component), Junior Leagues, etc.
- Business Partnerships
- Grass Roots Fundraising
- Individual sponsorship

Liability Issues. The best advice is to discuss this issue thoroughly with the school's or school district's legal advisor. Have clear written procedures and policies that reduce risk and danger, including parent permission forms, clear and adequate supervision and training, and insurance. Strong links to academic curriculum and the school's mission must be evident. Check on coverage of the agency where students are placed, as well as with large national insurance companies that specialize in insuring volunteers.

Transportation. Transportation need not be a major roadblock. There are numerous examples of middle level service learning projects where students never leave the classroom or school. In a situation where students cannot leave the school, such projects as cross-age tutoring, hospitality teams welcoming community members into the school, mentoring students new to the middle school, making art projects for nursing homes, and so on, can be utilized. Many senior citizen centers have their own transportation and can bring residents to the middle schools on a regular basis (Andrus and Joiner, 1989).

Students can also walk or use mass transportation, and school district vans or buses can be reserved. Perhaps a local business partner, service organization, or automobile dealership will donate a leased van.

Teacher Commitment. One of the most difficult challenges facing teachers is the limited time to accomplish all that has been asked of them. It is important that teachers realize that service learning is not just "one more thing" demanded of them, but is a proactive and effective method of instruction with high pay-offs. Student motivation, authentic assessment, student achievement, and attendance will increase through the use of service learning. In fact, many problems associated with student discipline and apathy will decrease. Strategies for staff implementation should include the following: (1) survey the staff to understand and learn about what is already occurring; (2) form a service learning action team comprised of those who are interested in this concept; (3) start small and build towards larger projects; (4) focus efforts on those enthusiastic about implementing service learning, not on those resistant to the idea; (5) have teachers visit sites with successful programs; (6) give mini-grants to help teachers get started; (7) provide resource materials and on-going staff development; and (8) have students, teachers, community representatives, community agency personnel, and parents do presentations about the service learning project complete with the components of preparation, integration, reflection, and evaluation.

Selected Service Learning Resources

Interest in service learning is on the rise. Educators and students are seeing great benefits from their involvement with service learning. There are several resources available on this subject which provide excellent information. Listed below are the resources and a short explanation about the contents of each.

- *The Service Learning Planning and Resource Guide,* by the Council of Chief State School Officers. Washington, D.C.: 1994. ISBN: 1-884037-04-6. Address: One Massachusetts Avenue, N.W., Suite 700, Washington, D.C. 20001; phone 202/408-5505; FAX 202/408-8072.

This outstanding 277 page resource guide provides information about funding sources for service learning. Included for each funding source is information about the agency, funding limits, and eligibility requirements. A short description of some of the projects and funding source is provided. This description will be helpful for those curious about the many different kinds of service learning projects being implemented throughout the United States. Another excellent aspect of this resource guide is the second section which provides information concerning service learning networks, the services they provide, and their publications. This useful, thoroughly prepared, and documented guide is a "must" for any school interested in service learning.

- *Growing Hope: A Sourcebook on Integrating Youth Service in the School Curriculum,* edited by R.W. Cairn and M.C. Kielsmeier. St. Paul, MN: National Youth Leadership Council, 1991. 1910 West County Road B., St. Paul, MN 55113; phone 612/631-3672.

  Growing Hope is another excellent resource. Included in this sourcebook is information about the many different kinds of service learning projects in practice. Provided are: (1) description of project; (2) information regarding implementation; (3) reflection exercises for each project; and (4) program contact addresses. Of particular interest to teachers are the sample program materials and resources used for each project, as well as the comprehensive listing of National Programs, Training Programs, NYLC Publications, National Service-Learning Initiative Regional Centers, Youth Service Organizations, and an extensive list of references.

- *Directory of Colorado Youth Service-Learning Programs,* by E. Andrus. Denver, CO: Colorado Department of Education, 1994. 201 E. Colfax Avenue, Denver, CO 80203; phone 303/866-6897.

  Colorado is a leader in service learning. Because of the commitment of The Colorado Department of Education to service learning, many schools are involved in service learning projects. This directory lists numerous schools that have integrated service learning into their educational experiences for students. Information contained in this document includes: (1) the name of the school, address, phone number, and contact person; and (2) a brief description of the service learning project.

In Conclusion

Service learning is an effective teaching and learning strategy. It includes *all* young adolescents in an active, learning environment. It is a valuable technique which can be used in systemic reform efforts and is being supported through national and state legislation and funding. When a middle school has implemented this kind of caring curriculum in a quality manner, students, staff members, parents, and the community all benefit greatly, for an integrated community of learners and learning has been achieved.

REFERENCES

Andrus, E. M., & Joiner, D. L. (1989). The community needs H.U.G.S.S. too!" *Middle School Journal,May,* 8–11.

Beane, J. A. (1993). *Middle school curriculum: From rhetoric to reality.* (2nd Ed.). Columbus, OH: National Middle School Association.

Boyer, E. L. (1983). *High school, a report on secondary education in America by the Carnegie Foundation for the Advancement of Teaching.* New York: Harper & Row.

Carnegie Council on Adolescent Development (1989). *Turning points: Preparing American youth for the 21st century.* New York, NY: Carnegie Corporation.

Cairn, R. W. (1993). Learning by giving: K–8 service learning curriculum guide. St. Paul, MN: National Youth Leadership Council.

Cairn, R., & Kielsmeier, J. C. (1991). *Growing hope: A sourcebook on integrating youth service into the school curriculum.* St. Paul, MN: National Youth Leadership Council.

Conrad, D., & Hedin, D. (1987). Learning from service. *Youth service: A guidebook for developing and operating effective programs.* Washington, D.C.: Independent Sector.

Learn and Serve America. (1994). *A resource guide for national and community service programs.* Washington, D.C.: The Corporation for National and Community Service.

Nathan, J., & Kielsmeier, J. (1991). The sleeping giant of school reform. *Phi Delta Kappan,* 72 (10), 5.

Sizer, T. R. (1992). *Horace's school.* Boston, MA: Houghton Mifflin.

CHAPTER 11

Selected Resources for Designing, Implementing, and Assessing Integrated Curriculum at the Middle Level

Barbara L. Whinery and John H. Swaim

The process of designing, developing, implementing, and evaluating integrated curriculum depends, in large part, on the use of a variety of resources. As steel and concrete are the materials used by engineers to construct bridges, so are resources such as people, professional organizations, and professional publications used by middle school educators as materials for developing effective integrated curricula.

Listed below are resources middle level educators can use when developing, implementing, and assessing integrated curricula. Notice, however, that not much has been published on curriculum integration, as defined in this book. The limited resources on middle level curriculum integration point to the fact that more needs to be written about this topic. Nevertheless, we have selected those resources we feel are important in this endeavor.

The Literature

The most current literature on middle level integrated curriculum has been defined by James Beane (1993) as something different from a multidisciplinary approach. Beane writes:

> Disenchantment with the "traditional" curriculum has led educators and others to begin moving away from the strict subject-centered approach. Many now talk about replacing subjects as organizing centers with "themes." But this does not tell us what those themes or their sources might be. Some speak of finding themes from existing curriculum that will encourage correlation across two or more subjects—what I refer to as a *multidisciplinary* approach. Others speak of

finding themes in social problems or in the issues facing young people in relation to development. In either case, some still use a multidisciplinary planning approach ("What can each subject area contribute?"), while others are willing to ignore subject area lines and instead draw from any subject area without regard for boundaries or identification, while focusing on the problem or issue at hand. This is what I would call *curriculum integration*, although that term has also been used with regard to "integrating" things like thinking, health, and writing across the subjects.

A few teachers (not enough, I think) are interested in planning the curriculum with young people in terms of questions and concerns they have about themselves and their world. In this case knowldge and skill are integrated naturally and by the young people themselves as they carry out their work. Experiences are integrated into present schemes of meaning and new ones are constructed. This I would call an *integrative curriculum* since the purpose is to help young people integrate their experiences on their own terms rather than those of adults (p. xiv).

Listed below are resources which reflect the current thinking on the curriculum integration at the middle level.

CURRICULUM INTEGRATION

* *A Middle School Curriculum: From Rhetoric to Reality* (2nd edition), by James Beane. Columbus, OH: National Middle School Association, 1993.

    This recent publication is a must for developing a sound philosophical foundation for integrating curriculum in middle schools. Beane honestly assesses the separate subject approach, and then discusses how an integrated curriculum that meets the developmental needs of young adolescents could be developed. He aptly presents a curriculum model that does not begin with subject matter areas, but rather starts with the questions and issues young adolescents have about their personal world and beyond.

* *Dissolving Boundaries: Toward an Integrated Curriculum,* by Edward Brazee and Jody Capelluti. Columbus, OH: National Middle School Association, 1995.

    This book will appeal to practitioners attempting to instigate significant curricular changes. The authors offer a solid rationale for curriculum integration, a specific planning process for implementing curriculum integration, and relections on what has worked in those schools which have been successful in implementing curriculum reform. In addition, seven stories by teams who have struggled with curriculum integration provide excellent illustrations that range from simple correlation through totally integrative curricula.

- *Integrated Studies in the Middle Grades: Dancing Through Walls,* by Chris Stevenson and Judith Carr. New York, NY: Teachers College Press, 1993.

  This book provides the reader with a well-stated philosophical rationale for integrated curriculum and instruction and why it is critical for the education of young adolescents. It also provides many practical examples of how integration can be used to teach young adolescents, written by the teachers who conducted them.

- *Making Connections: Teaching and The Human Brain,* by Renate Nummela Caine and Geoffrey Caine. Addison-Wesley, 1993.

  This seminal publication provides a scientific basis from brain research for the integration of the curriculum. The authors suggest that education should optimize the capacity of the human brain to make connections—to search for patterns rather than trying to understand isolated pieces of knowledge.

- Theme Issues on "Middle School Curriculum," edited by Tom Dickinson.

  Middle School Journal, Volume 23, Number 2, 1991.

  Middle School Journal, Volume 23, Number 3, 1992.

  Middle School Journal, Volume 26, Number 2, 1994.

  The National Middle School Association has published three feature issues on integrated middle school curriculum. A recurring theme in almost all of the articles in these featured issues is the support for integrated curriculum at the middle level and how this approach can be implemented. Authors include well-known authorities and practicing teachers.

- Theme Issue on "Integrating the Curriculum," edited by Ron Brandt. *Educational Leadership*, Volume 49, Number 2, 1991.

This issue includes a variety of articles that discuss the development and implementation of interdisciplinary curriculum. Featured are articles by leading authors Beane, Vars, Aschbacher, Drake, Brandt, and Jacobs in the field of curriculum.

- *We Gain More Than We Give: Teaming in Middle Schools,* by Thomas S. Dickinson and Thomas O. Erb. Columbus, OH: National Middle School Association (in press).

   This edited book of 26 chapters provides the reader with several ethnographic studies of middle teams, including long-term teams, teams in rural middle schols, and new teams in urban areas. One section of the book explores and elaborates on the research knowledge base for teaming. New challenges and possiblities are offered concerning curriculum integration, inclusion, site-based management, and whole langauge in the middle school.

- *Whole Learning in the Middle School: Evolution and Transition,* edited by Glennellen Pace. Norwood, MA: Christopher-Gordon, 1995.

   This book gives a clear, honest definition of whole learning as an evolutionary process. Helpful organization and management tips are given throughout the book regarding the establishment of a learner-centered classroom. Actual teachers experiences from different school settings, such as urban, small town, rural, self-contained, school-within-a-school, traditional blended age groups, collaborative team-teaching, and more, are featured. In addition, examples of student writing and dialogue are shared.

- For resources specific to instructional materials in reading and writing for middle level students, see Chapters 6 and 8.

OTHER RESOURCES

Literature from general curriculum study specific to interdisciplinary curriculum, as well as literature specific to the middle level, are significant. They have helped middle school educators move toward the concept of curriculum integration. Listed below are resources which we feel have contributed significantly to the middle school curriculum integration movement.

- *Connecting the Curriculum Through Interdisciplinary Instruction,* edited by John Lounsbury. Columbus, OH: National Middle School Association, 1992.

  Building a case for interdisciplinary instruction at the middle level including research results and procedures for planning, is the focus of the first two sections of this book. The third section provides examples of interdisciplinary curriculum, while the last section gives examples of how to implement interdisciplinary learning experiences in middle school classrooms.

- *Curriculum Planning and Development,* by James Beane, Conrad Toepfer, and Samuel Alessi. Boston, MA: Allyn and Bacon, 1986.

  This general curriculum textbook presents a framework for planning middle school curriculum. In Chapter 5 (pp. 141–178), the authors discuss four different approaches used in making decisions about the curriculum. These approaches include the following: subject-area (specific disciplines of knowledge); broad fields (broad ideas and concepts from subject fields); social problems (curriculum organized around major problems in society; i.e., environment, the future, racism); and needs of the young adolescent (personal and social needs, such as, personal values, peer relations, and physical development).

- *Designing Interdisciplinary Curriculum in Middle, Junior High and High Schools, by Richard E. Maurer. Boston, MA: Allyn and Bacon, 1993.*

  This guide to curriculum development presents the background and terminology of interdisciplinary curriculum, the elements of design, team organization, and sample interdisciplinary units.

- *Interdisciplinary Curriculum: Design and Implementation,* by Heidi Jacobs. Alexandria, VA: Association for Supervision and Curriculum Development, 1989.

  A continuum of design options for interdisciplinary curriculum, a description of two existing programs, and a step-by-step process for developing an interdisciplinary curriculum are presented in this book.

- "Interdisciplinary Curriculum in Middle School," by Dianne

Rothenberg. In *Middle School Journal*, Volume 25, Number 4, 1994, pp. 61-65.

This column provides annotated references of journal articles and ERIC documents that discuss the interdisciplinary approach to curriculum with a variety of content areas; i.e., mathematics, language arts, social studies, and the use of technology.

- *Interdisciplinary Inquiry in Teaching and Learning,* by Marian Martinello and Gillian Cook. New York, NY: Macmillan College Publishing Company, 1994.

  This book includes historical perspectives on interdisciplinary curriculum, guidelines for designing thematic studies, a variety of learning activities, methods of questioning, approaches to meeting the standards in different disciplines, use of resources, and strategies for implementation.

- *Interdisciplinary Teaching: Why and How?* (2nd ed.), by Gordon Vars. Columbus, OH: National Middle School Association, 1993.

  This outstanding book defines terminology and processes associated with the development of interdisciplinary curriculum. It also suggests an integrated approach which the author refers to as *core* curriculum. This is a valuable source of ideas and encouragement for individual teachers, teams, and facilities as they grapple with ways to break away from separate subject instruction.

- "Interdisciplinary Team Development in the Middle School: The Delta Project" by Laurie Hart, *et. al*. In *Research on Middle Level Education*, Volume 16, Number 1, Fall, 1992, pp. 79–98.

  This study describes four middle school teachers as they worked together with the same students on an interdisciplinary team over a period of three years.

- *Middle School Science and Technology Materials,* by The Biological Science Curriculum Study (BSCS). Dubuque, IA: Kendall-Hunt, 1994.

  These materials link the various areas of science, and integrate lifelong learning skills as an integral part of all activities which have been suggested. Themes such as patterns, diversity, and systems are discussed, along with instructional strategies and materials.

- *Planning Integrated Curriculum: The Call to Adventure,* by Susan M. Drake. Alexandria, VA: Association for Supervision and Curriculum Development, 1993.

  This monograph provides the rationale, process, and framework for designing and developing multidisciplinary, interdisciplinary, and transdisciplinary curricula. These approaches focus primarily on the diciplines and what happens to them as different organizing centers are used to develop the curriculum. The monograph provides a discussion of the experiences encountered by educators when developing interdisciplinary curriculum.

- *Readings in Middle School Curriculum: A Continuing Discussion,* edited by Tom Dickinson. Columbus, OH: National Middle School Association, 1993.

  A collection of readings by current writers in the field of middle school curriculum and their positions about the state of the curriculum and instructional practices at the middle level.

- *Research and Educational Innovations,* by Arthur K. Ellis and Jeffrey T. Fouts. Princeton Junction, NJ: Eye on Education, 1993.

  In Chapter 12, Ellis and Fouts present and discuss the movement toward an interdisciplinary approach to curriculum. The authors outline the reasons for shifting to such an approach. They emphasize the importance of student/teacher planning of this curriculum, and outline six claims advocates of interdisciplinary curriculum suggest as outcomes to using this approach.

- *The Exemplary Middle School* (2nd ed.), by Paul George and William Alexander. Fort Worth, TX: Harcourt Brace Jovanovich College Publishers, 1993.

  This book provides the history, theory, and philosophy of the middle school curriculum. It presents the components of an exemplary middle school curriculum as defined by the authors, along with a design of those components, examples of exemplary practices, and extensive reference lists for each.

- Theme Issue on "Middle Level Curriculum," edited by David Strahan and Brenda Leake. In *Research on Middle Level Education*, Volume 16, Number 2, Spring, 1993.

In this theme issue, there are a variety of studies concerned with interdisciplinary and integrated curriculum at the middle school level. Excellent resource for lending credibility to an integrated curriculum for middle school students and learning about the power and outcomes of an integrated curriculum.

- *The Mindful School: How to Integrate the Curricula,* by Robin Fogarty. Pallantine, IL: Skylight Publishing, 1991.

   This book presents 10 different models for curriculum development. A step-by-step approach is included for each model of development. This book will help the educator move from the traditional, separate, subject model through the interdisciplinary stage to curriculum integration.

- "Transforming Middle Level Education," by Judith Irvin. (Chapter 16). In *Transforming Middle Level Education: Perspectives and Possibilities,* edited by Judith Irvin. Needham, MA: Allyn and Bacon, 1992.

   This book contains a collection of readings written by prominent middle level educators on issues related to transforming middle schools from where they are to what they can become. Chapter 16, by Dr. Irvin, deals directly with developmentally appropriate instruction and interdisciplinary curriculum at the middle school level.

- *Using Curriculum Frameworks for Systematic Reform,* by Brian Curry and Tierney Temple. Alexandria, VA: Association for Supervision and Curriculum Development, 1992.

   This monograph explains and defines the concept of "curriculum frameworks" and how it applies to learning. It outlines guiding principles for developing frameworks, one of which addresses interdisciplinary curriculum.

GENERAL TEACHING STRATEGIES

As with the integrated curriculum, there are few resources which describe or present integrated instructional strategies. However, there are a few publications which present instructional models and strategies that are appropriate for young adolescents and middle level practice. Listed below are several such resources:

- *Dynamite in the Classroom, A How-To Handbook for Teachers,* by Sandra Schurr. Columbus, OH: National Middle School Association, 1989.

  This book presents teaching tips for teachers to improve their instruction in the middle school classroom. Teaching tips related specifically to curriculum integration are presented in Chapter 3.

- *Models of Teaching,* by Bruce Joyce and Marsha Weil. Boston, MA: Allyn and Bacon, 1992.

  The latest edition of this classic presents research-based models of instruction that facilitate the development of the learning environments and processes that are effective with students. Teachers can select a single model for a specific use or use a combination of models in an integrated curriculum.

- *Practical Strategies for Improving Instruction,* by Karen Wood. Columbus, OH: National Middle School Association, 1994.

  Twenty-three specific teaching strategies are described in this book. The strategies, all based on cited research, are oranized in a how-to format so that teachers can readily implement them in their classrooms. The strategies presented in the book cover such topics as assessment of reading and writing, cooperative learning, viewing, not taking, oral reading, integrative writing, reading for pleasure, improving vocabulary, and improving comprehension.

THE HUMAN ELEMENT

A critical component when integrating the curiculum is the group dynamic experienced by the teachers and students. The literature selected below describes team development and group processes:

- *Joining Together: Group Theory and Group Skills,* by David Johnson and Frank Johnson. Englewood Cliffs, NJ: Prentice Hall, 1991.

  The authors provide the theory and research on group development and dynamics. In this book, they also provide information regarding the development of group and individual interactional skills necessary when team teaching.

- *Team Organization: Promise-Practices and Possibilities,* by Thomas Erb and Nancy Doda. Washington, D.C.: National Education Association, 1989.

This book includes information about team implementation, team building, setting agenda, and teaching interdisciplinary units. It also identifies the characteristics and steps in planning thematic units.

- *The Team Process: A Handbook for Teachers* (3rd Ed.), by Elliot Merenbloom. Columbus, OH: National Middle School Association, 1991.

    This book outlines the process for implementing teaming in the middle school. It provides information about how teamwork affects curriculum development and addresses a variety of issues such as conflict resolution, team operations, and decision-making.

- *Working Together: Fundamentals of Group Decision Making,* by Rudolph Verderber. Belmont, CA: Wadsworth Publishing, 1982.

    In this book, Verderber offers excellent strategies for developing a cohesive and effective group. He discusses group decision-making models and processes, leadership responsibilities, individual and group roles, and evaluation. This book is filled with essential knowledge and skills needed to develop and implement teaming and integrated curriculum.

Assessment and Evaluation: Informing One's Teaching

On-going, formative and summative assessments are essential components of an integrated curriculum. Students should be able to demonstrate what they know and are able to do as they progress through learning experiences. Feedback on their performance will assist the teacher on modifying the curriculum and instructional approaches. With an integrated curriculum, there must be a variety of assessments which reflect the integrated nature of the curriculum and are appropriate to young adolescents. Authentic assessments such as portfolios and performance assessments (projects, debates, videos, etc.) are recommended. Also, two levels of assessment must be dealt with when implementing integrated curriculum. One is at the program level and the other involves individual students. Both must be addressed if the curriculum is to be deemed effective and accountable. However, resources presented here will focus only on formative teacher evaluation and assessment of individual students. A variety of strategies must be selected for both formative and summative assessments.

With education moving toward a standards-based curriculum and authentic assessments, consideration of national and state standards are extremely important when designing and developing performance assessments. Another consideration should be the appropriateness of the assessment to the young adolescent.

Besides focusing on student learning, teachers are empowered when they are able to examine their own teaching. Thus, we feel including information about the teacher as researcher is imperative. When teachers do research about their own teaching, the learning that occurs is phenomenal. Teachers learn about important matters such as: What matters most in the classroom? What kinds of things matters most to students? What strategies seem to help students learn?

INDIVIDUAL STUDENT ASSESSMENT

- *A Guide to Alternative Assessment,* by Joan Herman, Pamela Aschbacher, and Lynn Winters. Alexandria, VA: Association for Supervision and Curriculum Development, 1992.

     This excellent resource presents guidelines for developing alternative assessments. Such things as linking assessment and instruction, selecting assessment tasks, setting criteria, and addressing the technical aspects of performance assessments are discussed.

- "Assessment: Authenticity, Context, and Validity," by Grant Wiggins. In *Phi Delta Kappan*, Volume 75, Number 3, 1993, pp. 200–214.

     This article provides a thorough discussion of the issues associated with assessment. An excellent resource for teachers, parents, and administrators.

- "Humanizing Student Evaluation and Reporting," by Gordon Vars. (Chapter 18). In *Transforming Middle Level Education: Perspectives and Possibilities,* edited by Judith Irvin. Needham, MA: Allyn and Bacon, 1992.

     Presents a review of the literature for student evaluation at the middle school level and provides the principles for developing a system that is responsive to the developmental characteristics of young adolescents.

- *Readings from Educational Leadership: Performance Assessment,* edited by Ronald Brandt. Alexandria, VA: Association for Supervision and Curriculum Development, 1992.

This book contains a collection of the most recent articles from *Educational Leadership* on the need for change in assessment practices, portfolio development, performance assessments, and the alignment of assessments to standards and desired student outcomes.

- Theme Issue on "Alternative Assessment," edited by Tom Dickinson. *Middle School Journal*, Volume 25, Number 2, 1993.

This entire issue is devoted to alternative assessment techniques that are appropriate to use with young adolescents. Articles include discussions of portfolios, use of authentic assessments, and alternative assessment procedures which can be used in an interdisciplinary or integrated curriculum.

- Theme Issue on "Using Performance Assessment," edited by Ron Brandt. *Educational Leadership*, Volume 49, Number 8, 1992.

This issue focuses on performance assessment portfolios and a synthesis of research on good assessment.

- Theme Issue on "The Challenge of Outcome-Based Education," edited by Ron Brandt. *Educational Leadership*, Volume 51, Number 6, 1994.

Articles in this theme issue present current practices in several school districts and discuss critical points associated with outcome-based education and assessment.

- Theme Issue on "Authentic Assessment," edited by Beverly Falk. *The Educational Forum*, Volume 59, Number 1, Fall, 1994.

Features articles focusing on assesment reform, accountibility, portfolio and video assessment, and theory into practice issues related to authentic assessment.

- *The ABC's of Evaluation: 26 Alternative Ways to Assess Student Progress,* by Sandra Schurr. Columbus, OH: National Middle School Association, 1992.

Examples of assessment approaches appropriate for middle level students are described A through Z.

TEACHER AS RESEARCHER

- *A Teacher's Guide to Classroom Research* (2nd ed.), by David Hopkins. Philadelphia: Open University Press, 1993.

  A very user friendly guide to designing and implementing action research in the classroom. Provides the basics in classroom observation, data gathering, and analyzing research data.

- *How to Conduct Collaborative Action Research,* by Richard Sagor. Alexandria, VA: Association for Supervision and Curriculum Development, 1993.

  Explains how collaborative reseach can build a positive climate for restructuring. Outlines a step by step process for conducting action research, research techniques for identifying and focusing on a problem, and methods for collecting valid and reliable data.

- *Using Educational Research in the Classroom* (Phi Delta Kappa Fastback), by Barbara Perry-Sheldon. Bloomington, ID: Phi Delta Kappa Foundation.

  Presents background information on classroom action research and discusses several models used in implementing classroom research. Strategies assist practicioners who are developing initial action research projects.

Curriculum Centers

Over the last decade, several centers have been established which deal directly with middle level education. These centers have provided a variety of services which have enhanced the development of middle level education at the state, national, and even international levels. They have sponsored research studies, hosted workshops and institutes, and served as a repository for material on middle level education. Likewise, there has been a growing number of projects funded through a variety of sources which have dealt directly with issues affecting middle level education.

The following is a list of some of the centers and projects which directly or indirectly provide information about middle school integrated curriculum and instruction. Many of the units are interdisciplinary, but can provide examples of possibilities. Keep in mind, however, that true curriculum integration happens within a context where teachers and students co-create curriculum; therefore, it is often difficult to truly integrate curricula when using other people's units of study.

- *Carnegie Council on Adolescent Development*, P.O. Box 753, Waldorf, MD 20604.

  The Council has provided funding for several projects related to the 1987 report *Turning Points: Preparing Youth for the Twenty First Century.* Some of these grants have directly or indirectly involved the promotion and/or study of interdisciplinary education at the middle school level.

- *Center for Early Adolescence*, University of North Carolina at Chapel Hill, D-2 Carr Mill Town Center, Carrboro, NC 27510.

  The Center was established to promote the study of young adolescents. Although much of the work of the Center has focused on the development of young adolescents, it has involved the education of young adolescents, including work on integrated curriculum and instruction.

- *Colorado Middle Level Interdisciplinary Center*, The University of Northern Colorado Laboratory School, Greeley CO, 80639.

  This self-supporting center is sponsored by the Colorado Association of Middle Level Education. It serves as a clearinghouse for teacher-made interdisciplinary units. Teachers who send in a unit will receive a free unit of their choice in return for contributing to the center. The Center has over 100 different units. The units may be purchased for the cost of duplication and postage. Catalogs listing the units may be attained from the address above.

- *National Resource for Middle Grades Education*, University of South Florida, Tampa, FL 33620-5650.

  This is the only comprehensive resource center on middle level education in the United States. The Center provides a wealth of materials on middle school education and sponsors various workshops related to various aspects of middle level education.

Professional Organizations and Journals

The professional associations and journals listed below are the most probable sources for finding information on integrated curriculum at the middle school level. This list only contains the professional associations and journals that have a national membership and/or distribution. It does not account for all the state middle school associations and publications which have also been active in the promotion of integration at the middle school level.

PROFESSIONAL ORGANIZATIONS

- *National Middle School Association*, 2600 Corporate Exchange Drive, Suite 370, Columbus, OH 43231.

   This is the only national professional education association whose sole focus is on middle level education. Its membership represents over 60,000 middle level educators.

- *New England League of Middle Schools*, 15 Summer Street, Rowley, MA 01969.

   A regional middle school association in the New England area that draws its membership from several of the New England states. It is the largest regional middle school association in the United States. It has promoted integration of curriculum and instruction through its publications, conferences, and workshops.

PROFESSIONAL JOURNALS

- *Educational Leadership*, Association for Supervision and Curriculum Development, 1250 Pitt St., Alexandria, VA 22314-1453.

   A journal of the Association for Supervision and Curriculum Development which focuses on information relevant to supervising teachers and developing curricula.

- *Middle School Journal,* National Middle School Association, 2600 Corporate Exchange Drive, Suite 370, Columbus, OH 43231.

   A journal that has established itself as the premiere middle school journal in the United States and Canada. It deals with a variety of issues in middle level education including integrated curriculum.

- *High Strides,* National Middle School Association, 2600 Corporate Exchange Drive, Suite 370, Columbus, OH 43231.

    This publication deals with middle level education in an urban setting. It often features articles on the integration of school and community.

- *Transescence: Journal on Emerging Adolescent Education,* edited by Conrad Toepfer, Educational Leadership Institute, Inc., Box 363, Springfield, MA 01101.

    This journal provides a forum for middle level advocates to express their point of view and take a stand on issues effecting middle level education.

- *Voices from the Middle,* National Council of Teachers of English, 1111 W. Kenyon Road, Urbana, IL 61801-1096.

    This new journal from NCTE is based on the premises that middle school teachers face unique challenges and that hearing from other middle school teachers about their successes, solutions, or concerns is helpful. Each themed issue begins with an article that explains the theoretical aspects of the topic. Then, the next three articles provide a look into classrooms where the theory is being explored and implemented. There is also a bibliography of suggested readings and reviews of trade books and professional books about the topic.

Developing New Bridges

This chapter has provided possible resources to support middle level educators in the design, development, implementation, and evaluation of an integrated middle school curriculum. There are still more bridges to be built and we need more knowledge of what works and what does not. More appropriate and authentic assessments need to be designed. Better ways to prepare and in-service teachers to meet the challenge of the integration of middle school curriculum need to be developed and implemented. Only then can we build an integrated, holistic curriculum that truly reflects the cognitive, social, emotional, and physical characteristics of the young adolescent. Continuous communication, coordination, and evaluation of our efforts will assist all those who are pushing the integrated curriculum agenda forward.

CONTRIBUTORS

Yvonne Siu-Runyan is an Associate Professor of Literacy at the University of Northern Colorado in Greeley, Colorado, where she teaches undergraduate and graduate courses in literacy development. She has taught grades K-12 in the states of Colorado, California, Hawaii, Michigan and Ohio. Currently, she is editor of *The Colorado Communicator* and is a member of review boards for *The International Reading Professional Books Publication, The Reading Teacher* and *The New Advocate*. Dr. Siu-Runyan has spoken widely and written book chapters and articles about whole language instruction, integrative learning, writing and reading instruction, children's literature, and supervision. In addition to chairing committees for IRA, NCTE, and CCIRA, she is a founding executive board member for the Whole Language Umbrella, an International Confederation of Teachers.

C. Victoria Faircloth received her Ed.D. from University of Georgia and is presently an Assistant Professor at Western Carolina University. Prior to working at the university level, she taught for eleven years at elementary and middle schools in Georgia. She has authored a number of professional articles including, "The Change Process in Interdisciplinary Teaching" and "Getting a Grip on Technology Education", which were both published in *Middle School Journal*. In addition, Dr.

Faircloth has presented dozens of middle school workshops and papers, on topics that include: the integrated curriculum, science awareness, change and teaming. In 1994, she gave the keynote address titled, "In the Middle and Lovin' It" at the North Carolina Middle School Association Fall Conference.

Harry E. Ashton (Bud) earned his BS in Secondary Education and his MA in Secondary Administration from Western Michigan University. After teaching and coaching at the elementary, junior high, and high school levels, he moved from the classroom to high school administration. As the principal of a junior high school in Winter Park, Colorado, he guided his staff in the introduction and implementation of the middle school concept. He and his staff became a lead school by participating in a federally funded project to develop interdisciplinary units, which led to him presenting on middle school change at numerous conferences and workshops. Currently, Mr. Ashton is a high school principal in Northern Michigan, where he is blending middle school practices into the high school and guiding the junior high staff in their transition to a middle school.

Elaine Andrus is the Director of the Carnegie Middle Level Grant Initiative for Colorado as well as the Director of Service Learning-Colorado. During her years as a middle level teacher, she "lived through" the transition process from a traditional junior high to the implementation of true middle level philosophy. She created and implemented the H.U.G.S.S. Program, a service learning model for middle schools, as well as programs for advisor-advisee and youth "at risk". She has consulted for several school districts and served on numerous committees at the national policy level in Washington, D.C.

James A. Beane is a Professor in the National College of Education at National-Louis University and the author of *Affect in the Curriculum: Toward Democracy, Dignity and Diversity* and *A Middle School Curriculum: From Rhetoric to Reality*. In addition, he has contributed chapters, articles, and forewords to a variety of books and journals. Dr. Beane has spoken at numerous national, state and local conferences, been a consultant for educational projects in the U.S. and elsewhere, and served in various capacities for several professional associations.

Edward N. Brazee is currently Associate Professor at the University of Maine, where he directs the Middle Level concentration of the Individualized Master's Degree and teaches graduate courses at the middle level. As a founder and director of the Middle Level Education Institute and the Maine Association for Middle Level Education, Dr. Brazee has worked with many middle level educators to devise and implement developmentally responsive programs for young adolescents. In addition, he is the past chairman of the Conferences and Institutes Committee of the National Middle School Association.

Norman Higgs, who has thirty-eight years of experience in education, is presently the principal of Smiley Middle School. His undergraduate degree is from Hardin Simmons University and he has a masters in educational administration from Adams State College. In 1990, he piloted the change from junior high to middle school in the Durango school district, and since then the Smiley Middle School has been recognized statewide as a leader in philosophy and curriculum integration. He and many of the teams at Smiley have been asked to present at various middle school conferences regarding "teaming" and techniques used to make middle school a success.

Tim Hillmer is a teacher in the CHOICE program at Platt Middle School in the Boulder Valley School District. He received his B.S. from Southern Illinois University-Edwardsville, and his M.S.T. from the University of New Hampshire. He has received awards for his teaching from the Colorado Language Arts Society and the Phi Delta Kappa chapter of the University of Colorado. In 1992 he was the recipient of a Creative Fellowship in Fiction from the Colorado Council on the Arts, and in 1993 his novel, *The Hookmen*, received the Colorado Fiction award. During the 1994-95 school year he is serving as a teacher scholar in the American Council of Learned Societies Elementary and Secondary School Curriculum Development Project.

Elaine Homestead is a teacher at Duluth Middle School in Duluth, Georgia, a suburb of Atlanta. She has 15 years teaching experience in grades five through eight. For the past two years she been part of a two-teacher eighth grade team, which focuses on collaborating with students to integrate social studies, science, language arts, math and the fine arts. A book about their efforts to create a problem-based, issues-oriented, student-centered curriculum is currently being written. She has

co-authored other publications including: a chapter in ASCD's 1995 Yearbook and two articles in the Middle School Journal. She was awarded an MEd in Middle Grades Education from the University of Georgia, and is currently working on her doctorate.

Janice V. Kristo is an Associate Professor of Literacy Education at the University of Maine, where she teaches
courses in reading and language arts
methods and children's literature. She
is an active member of the Children's
Literature Assembly of the National
Council of Teachers of English, having
served as chair of the Notable Trade
Books in the Language Arts Committee.
She is the co-editor of *Inviting Children's
Responses to Literature: Guides to 57
Notable Books* and the forth-coming

texts, *Booktalk: Books that Invite Talk. Wonder and Play with Language* and
Teaching Integrated Language Arts: Process and Practice. In addition, she
has published numerous articles and chapters on her research in whole
language classrooms and appears on many national convention programs.

Bernie Martinez has been involved in ed-
ucation at many levels over the past 25
years. He served as Director of Bilingual
Education and regional Director for Civil
Rights Training Center for the Colorado
Department of Education. After teaching
Spanish at Valley High School for several
years, he became Assistant Principal at
Valley High School. In 1984, Bernie
became Principal at South Valley Middle
School and has been involved with the
Northern Colorado Summer Migrant
Program. He resides in Greeley, Colorado.

Karen McGinnis is a teacher at Duluth Middle School in Duluth, Georgia, a suburb of Atlanta. She has 7 years experience in middle grades education in departmentalized, exploratory, interdisciplinary team, and integrated settings. For the past two years she has been part of a two-teacher eighth grade team, which aimed to integrate the curriculum in collaboration with students. A book about their efforts within this team is currently being written. Karen has co-authored other publications including: a chapter in ASCD's 1995 Yearbook: *Toward a Coherent Curriculum* and two articles in the Middle School Journal. In 1994, she was awarded a MEd in Middle Grades Education from the University of Georgia.

Richard Needham has taught at the elementary, middle and secondary level and is presently an Associate Professor of Elementary Education at the University of Northern Colorado, where he teaches elementary school curriculum and social studies. He has conducted workshops and seminars across the U.S. and in Canada, Australia and Kenya. He has authored numerous articles and has been active in professional organizations including IRA and NCSS. His current interests include integrated curriculum, children's literature, authentic instruction and assessment, and standards-based education.

P. Elizabeth Pate is an Associate Professor in the Elementary Education Department, Middle School Program, at The University of Georgia. She completed her Ph.D. in Curriculum and Instruction at Texas A&M University in 1989. Prior to graduate school, she taught at the elementary and middle school levels. She is involved in several research studies focusing on middle level education, including curriculum integration and strategy instruction. She is currently the president of the Middle Level Special Interest Group, American Educational Research Association.

Deborah Ann Powell is a curriculum consultant for Mimosa Publications, Melbourne, Australia. She has been a teacher for over 25 years in the elementary and middle school, and as an Associate Professor of reading and elementary education at the University of Northern Colorado. She is co-author of *Learning Phonics and Spelling in a Whole Language Classroom* and has written numerous articles for teacher, and eight poetry collections for children in Rigby's *Literacy 2000* series. She has conducted teacher workshops internationally and was co-director of the Elementary Science Implementation Project funded by the National Science Foundation.

Elizabeth J. Robinson is presently a Language Arts teacher and drama coach at The Leonard Middle School in Old Town, Maine, where there are approximately 350 students in grades six through eight. Her past teaching experience includes both kindergarten and elementary school. She received her undergraduate and graduate degrees from the University of Maine at Orono, where she has been an Instructor for the past five years. In addition, she is a seminar leader at the American Institute for Creative Education in Augusta, Maine.

John H. Swaim is a Professor Emeritus from the University of Northern Colorado. He is the past president of the National Middle School Association and was the first president and charter member of the Colorado Association of Middle Level Education. He is also the recipient of the National Middle School Association Distinguished Service Award.

Barbara Whinery is an Assistant Professor in the Middle School Education Program at the University of Northern Colorado. She has presented at state, regional, and national middle school conferences. Her research interests include middle school instruction, integrated curriculum and teacher education. She is actively involved with the development of the undergraduate and graduate middle school teacher education programs at the University of Northern Colorado.

INDEX